Praise for
52 Weeks to Self-Love

There is a lot of talk about the importance of loving oneself but for most of us, those are words that have little meaning. They sound lovely but what, exactly, do they mean in the day to day? *52 Weeks to Self-Love* is a wonderful guide to anyone wanting to live a more conscious and confident life. Each week is organized to help us to reflect on the topic, explore how we can use this understanding, and ends with an exercise to bring the work to life. All of this with beautiful, evocative images. Dr. Gionta has a way of weaving together her expertise as a psychologist, with her personal life experiences, and the wisdom from listening to others.

Self-love can genuinely change the world. Don't just read this book, do the exercises, share what you are learning, and invite others to join you on this journey.

— Linda J. Carpenter, PhD (she/her)
Founding Partner and Senior Consultant,
Carpenter Smith Consulting

In her compelling book, *52 Weeks to Self-Love*, Dr. Dana Gionta presents a transformative journey that is essential for women who seek to cultivate a stronger relationship with themselves, and embrace a more present and peaceful life.

Dr. Dana provides readers with actionable insights and exercises designed to develop greater self-love and confidence. What truly stands out in this book is Dr. Gionta's genuine sharing of her own journey. Her vulnerability fosters a deep connection with readers, making her strategies not only relatable but also highly effective. The gentle and compassionate tone of her writing creates a safe space for women to explore their feelings and experiences, paving the way for profound healing. A must-have for clinicians and individuals ready to embark on a beautiful journey of self-discovery, love, and empowerment. Highly recommend!
— Medina Cecunjanin, LCSW

52 Weeks to Self-Love is filled with powerful strategies in our journey toward greater love, compassion and understanding of ourselves. The weekly themes, practices and reflections narrow the focus for readers. The depth of the content is balanced by the gentleness of author Dr. Dana Gionta's approach and personal anecdotes shared along the way.

It is a fantastic tool to cultivate a deeper, more loving relationship with oneself, and will help you live your life the way you really want to live it!"
— Jill Brazier
Teacher and Organizing Consultant

Dr. Dana Gionta dives heroically into the shallows, where we merely wet our feet to keep us from experiencing the exhilaration of purposefully gliding free-style into the depths of our magnificent selves.

As she empowers us with expert direction and vital questions, we find not only self-love, but a path to peace, and along the way we learn many strategies to connect with our feelings, and most importantly, our Selves.

Treasure this book, and you will never be in the shallows again.

— Elizabeth Anne Cooper
Retired president and CEO,
Princeton Insights Advertising.

This book is such a practical, heartfelt approach to becoming your best self. Dana leads each section with important insights, followed by a lean in with curiosity to help us reflect more deeply. I love how she connects everything back to our daily lives, and offers steps we can take to make even the smallest changes for the biggest impact. So grateful for this resource as I continue my personal growth journey, one week at a time!

— Joan Green
Director of Talent Acquisition

52 Weeks to Self-Love is a must read for all women seeking to find balance and prioritize a loving relationship with themselves and others.

Dr. Gionta integrates thought provoking questions in an easy-to-use workbook format, and shares stories from her own personal life experiences. Dr. Dana guides us to put into practice self-care techniques, set healthy boundaries, pursue life goals, and feel proud of who we are. I highly recommend this book!

— Barb Pfister
Health Care Provider

Comforting, thought provoking, and insightful, this book will change the way you view not only yourself, but also how you interact with the people in your everyday life. It is beautifully written, easy to understand, and is a book that will stay with you long after you finish reading it! Dana takes you on a journey that will shift your perspective on how you perceive life. Would highly recommend this to anyone looking to embrace themselves and find strength in their vulnerability.

— Keiko Arizala, Ph.D.

From the very first pages to the last, Dr. Gionta provides a transformative experience with weekly thought-provoking explorations and gently guided steps that lead to a deeper connection with yourself, and to a healthy and joyful life. Take time for yourself, and go on this beautiful year long journey. You will come out a changed woman with insight, clear boundaries, a newfound self-awareness and Love! YOU ARE WORTH IT!

— Susan Di Pasquale RN, MS
Organizer, Summerlin Socializing Sisters Group

Dr. Dana Gionta takes on the elusive concept of "self-love" and breaks it down into manageable, actionable activities that teach us how to have a loving, honoring relationship with ourselves. Through the guided journal format of this book, she has created the safe space we all need to dive deeper into our inner worlds by allowing for our authentic thoughts, feelings and yearnings to exist. Dr. Gionta's warmth, encouragement, validation, and genuine belief in the reader is felt throughout the book and will bring you the courage to keep moving forward, knowing she is there by your side, cheering you on. Easy to read and practical, yet highly effective and truly life changing, this is a book you will return to time and time again.

— Holly Spotts, Psy.D.
Founder, Full Cup Wellness Therapy for Women

52 Weeks to Self-Love provides guidance on one of the most important journeys you can embark on—the journey to self-love. Beautifully written, this book is filled with practical exercises and reflections that will change the way you feel about yourself. It is an excellent guide and a go-to resource to build your confidence, get unstuck, and live a more courageous life.

— Sunni Lampasso, PsyD
Founder & CEO, Shaping Success LLC

52 WEEKS TO
SELF-LOVE

52 WEEKS TO
SELF-LOVE

A Yearlong Journey of Inspirational and
Empowering Reflections for Women

DANA A. GIONTA PH.D.

Las Vegas, Nevada
Barricella Press

Ordering information: Special rates are available on quantity purchases by corporations, associations and others. For details, please direct inquiries to: www.barricellapress.com

Published by:

BP
Barricella Press
Las Vegas, Nevada
www.barricellapress.com

Paperback ISBN: 979-8-9912535-0-5
Hardcover ISBN: 979-8-9912535-1-2
Ebook ISBN: 979-8-9912535-2-9
Library of Congress Control Number (LCCN): 2024917394

Book design by Journey Bound Publishing

10 9 8 7 6 5 4 3 2 1
First edition

This book is dedicated to all the women who are on their own beautiful and courageous journey to a Loving relationship with them Selves. I believe it is the greatest gift you can give your Self, and those you love.

Acknowledgements

I n the chapters ahead, there is a reflection on Joy. I never imagined sitting down to write could bring such joy, until I began writing these reflections. Perhaps because I've come to experience them as being written through me by Divine Source—to share her wisdom, compassion, and love with you.

I would also like to share a heartfelt thanks to all of those who helped bring this book to you. Their expertise, dedication, encouragement and support made this all possible.

Lorenza Barricella, for your technical savvy and intuitive creative gifts, making the initial formatting and publishing process of this book feel almost seamless. Your wonderful attitude, attention to detail, and professionalism made working together a delight!

Veronica Yager, Cheryl Callighan and the team at Journey Bound Publishing for your expertise, professionalism, creative talents, and marketing savvy which have been invaluable in bringing *52 Weeks to Self-Love* to women around the world.

Daria Hong, whose editing finesse and consistent encouragement led to the beautiful crafting and flow of these reflections.

Sunni Lampasso and Joan Green, my incredible accountability partners, our regular meetings were invaluable in helping me maintain enthusiasm and momentum in bringing *52 Weeks to Self-Love* to the finish line. A success indeed!

Saheran Shoukat, for the beautiful cover design, capturing the essence of a woman's journey of Self-discovery and Love.

Suzanne Harle, whose design talents shined while helping me add an invaluable finishing touch to the book cover.

Susan, and the Summerlin Socializing Sisters, who took the time to select their favorite book titles and cover, and enthusiastically shared the importance of my work. Grateful for your support and enthusiasm!

And to my clients over the years who I've had the honor to work with, learn from, and walk beside on their life-changing journey to greater Self-love and confidence.

Contents

The Landscape of Your Mind

On Living Consciously

Prioritize Your Happiness

Holidays

Navigating Life Stress

Empower Your Self

Taking Action

Faith & Beyond

Let Go of Perfection and Get Unstuck

Introduction

t is my deep joy in sharing *52 Weeks to Self-Love* with you. I hope your year long spiritual journey is everything you hope it will be and more! I've come to believe that our growth mirrors that of a beautiful garden. We often don't see the incredible movement and changes happening within the soil below, until the first blossoms appear. Our transformation is similar. We often go weeks and months without seeing any visible signs of progress until "suddenly" outward changes appear.

Along your journey through this book, you may not see any visible changes for several weeks or longer. It is very important for you to let go of any expectations, as best you can, and Trust the process. Change is happening. Remember the garden metaphor. And if you get discouraged, that's okay. It's part of the process of growth. Bring kindness and compassion to your Self. Continue to journal and apply as many of the reflections that resonate with you. You will be amazed at the beautiful woman who is You blossoming into full bloom over the months ahead...

Much of what is written in the chapters ahead comes also from my coaching and therapy work with my clients over the past 20 years. It's been wonderful, even amazing at times, to consistently see how transformative these reflections are when practiced.

Because of this I know that if you embrace these reflections, make time to journal in the pages ahead, and put into practice the concepts and ways of being over the weeks ahead—you will indeed develop a loving and compassionate relationship with your Self, and feel greater confidence, courage, and peace in your life overall. What a wonderful gift to give your Self! Let's begin this extraordinary journey…

Dana Gionta

Your Relationship with Your Self

"If I have a deeper relationship with myself, my roots go downwards toward an intrinsic sense of worth, not outward toward an extrinsic search for validation…"

— JOHN NILAND

01
A Friendship with Your Self

Our relationship with ourselves is the most important relationship we'll ever have in our lives. How we treat ourselves is often reflective of how we likely treat others. If we are kind to and supportive of ourselves, we will show others this caring behavior also. If we judge ourselves with "shoulds" and "have to's," or hold ourselves to unrealistic standards, it's very likely we will do this with others in our lives.

Pause and Consider These Questions:

Do you more often give your Self the gift of compassion and acceptance or the weight of self-judgment?

Do you talk to your Self in kind and respectful ways, like a good friend, or harshly, often with hurtful words?

Do you frequently compare your Self to others, and come away feeling less than, or do you see your unique strengths and celebrate what you have accomplished?

Do you listen to and honor your feelings, or judge them (or yourself for having such feelings), and try to push them away?

Do you make time for your Self to relax, renew, laugh, have fun, and enjoy the many beautiful gifts life has to offer? Or do you prioritize responsibilities and obligations, and squeeze in You time at the end of the day, if possible?

When you begin caring for your Self in nurturing ways, something magical starts to happen. Like seeds planted in a beautiful garden, with each step, or kind thought—you are cultivating a positive and loving connection with You. Over time, the gifts of this begin to unfold.

Some Ways to Be Better Friends with Our Selves

Consider spending more alone time with your Self. Think about how you would like to spend this time, what would you enjoy? What would light up your spirit, warm your heart, or bring you peace? Then select one, and carve out some time this week to experience this.

Were you able to enjoy being with your Self, your own company? If yes, great! If not, that's okay. Reflect on what contributed to it being less enjoyable. Then identify one small shift you can make to have a better experience next time, and be more of a loving friend toward your Self.

This week, pretend you have an imaginary friend with you for the week. What would she notice about your relationship with your Self—kindness, positivity, and humor sprinkled throughout each day? Or more judgments, blame, and comparisons happening? If the latter, what would this loving imaginary friend share with you about how you can be kinder to your Self?

Notes:

_____

_____

_____

_____

02
The Currency of Love

Love in its essence, is pure, simple, and one of most powerful healing forces in life. Often though, it gets distorted with our own very human fears, egos, learned behaviors, traumas, and beliefs about what it "should" be. Our families, society, and childhood all significantly shape our concept and understanding of what Love is, and what a loving relationship looks like.

We each have what I like to call a "currency" of love which we've learned from our family dynamics growing up. For some, that currency is always "doing" for others or "being available to listen and give emotional support" as a way to get some positive attention and caring from family members. For others, it's being the 'strong one" or the family "caregiver"—always tending to others' needs and problems to receive some attention and love in return. Others may have served as the family jokester, troublemaker, or peace-keeper. Take a moment, and notice if any of the roles or patterns above resonate? Consider which one or two you may have taken on in your family. This takes some courage.

Identifying our currency is helpful because often times we continue this into our relationships in young adulthood and throughout our lives, if we're not aware. However, once we identify this, it's both empowering and freeing to get to choose how we want to Be and Relate to others in our adult life. We can then determine for our Selves what Loving and "to love" means to us in a more conscious and intentional way.

Reflections on Loving

What does loving look like for you in relation to those closest to you? How do you most often express it—through words, actions, gestures of affection, or doing for? Do others in your life experience your love for them…do they feel loved by you? If so, wonderful! If not, ask your Self what factors may be getting in the way? Consider identifying each other's love language to express love in ways that are received the way you intend.

Notice how your ways of loving feel for You. Are the loving behaviors and expressions most often given freely and genuinely? Do they feel nourishing, uplifting and perhaps heart-warming for you? Or are feelings of resentment and frustration with a sense of obligation and shoulding more common? Are your relationships in general reciprocal with a sense of balance, so you feel you are also receiving love and care? This is an important aspect of a healthy relationship.

And last, but definitely not least, is a loving relationship with your Self. In what ways do you show love and kindness to your Self? Notice how you talk, behave and think about your Self—your abilities, personal qualities, intelligence, humor, body, and past decisions etc. What are some stories you often share with others about your Self. Do they lean more positive or negative?

This week, observe your Self showing love to others and see if you can identify your key currency of love? Notice how engaging in this currency feels for you. If it feels free, by choice, and nourishing, then happily continue it. If it feels somehow familiar, restricting, or some frustration is present, then just let your Self Be in that moment...without that currency... in whatever way feels nurturing to you. Watch the wonders that often come when we do!

Notes:

_____

_____

_____

_____

03
Believe in You

One of the greatest gifts we can give to our Selves is the belief in our Selves—our goodness, abilities, resilience, needs, uniqueness and dreams. Often though, we learn to doubt and question our Selves through our family dynamics and roles, school and work experiences, and societal dictates about what is "right, good or normal." This results in us turning outside our Selves to others for answers about our lives. We may frequently check with our friends or family before making a decision, or do a poll asking others' opinions about something. Less often do we tune inward and ask our Selves what we really think, feel, or intuit about a situation. And if we do, we often don't trust it, and indirectly, our Selves.

The etymology of believe is "to have faith and confidence in" and "to care, love." When others question us and show little faith in our abilities or dreams, we have an important choice to make. Do we choose to believe them (and give our power and what matters to us away) or do we choose to have faith in our Selves. The latter shows care and love toward our Selves. Life is filled with much uncertainty. Learning to trust and believe in our Selves makes navigating the unchartered terrain and twists and turns easier, and with greater calm. It also allows us to take risks and live more courageously because we believe in our Selves. We know we are resilient and resourceful.

Some Ways to Strengthen The Belief in Our Selves

Notice how often self-doubt comes up for you. Is it daily, weekly? Consider writing down for one week each thought of self-doubt that comes up, and then identify if there are specific themes or decisions that trigger the self-doubt. For example, you notice any time a money matter arises, self-doubt also is present. This is valuable information. What is one action you can take to develop greater confidence in your ability around money matters (hint: start where your fear is).

Tune in more to the communication and resulting messages you receive from loved ones, friends, co-workers, etc. Do they convey faith in you, perhaps even admiration for your problem-solving and overall abilities? Or do they frequently question you, your ideas/approach, and proceed to tell you their "better way." Notice how you feel during and after each type of exchange. Then give your Self permission to do it your way, and evaluate the outcome. What worked well, and what would you do differently the next time? Confidence comes through action, and building self-trust.

This week, reflect and identify a time (or decision) in your life when you really believed in your Self. How did it feel, what were you doing, and what factors supported your confidence in your Self at that time? Consider which of those factors are still present in your life now. If not many, which 1-2 aspects could you reintegrate into your life to support giving your Self this wonderful gift of Believing?

_____

_____

_____

_____

04
It's All About Love

O ften, there are many competing demands for
our time and attention. The pressure to succeed—whatever that may look like for you, and
to accomplish our goals and to become a better person is
ever present. Sometimes we feel overwhelmed by it all, and
wonder what's really important, and where to focus our
energy. It can be confusing and stressful to sort through
and uncover our truth around this.

I recently had a personal experience that felt spiritual.
I was attending a virtual event around increasing our
visibility and influence. As we were sharing the inherent
challenges many experienced around this, the theme of
self-acceptance and the emotion of fear frequently arose.
We all want to belong, fit in and be accepted, and avoid
judgement and rejection.

Unexpectedly, as I was listening, this extraordinary
wave of love washed over me, and around me, and the
wisdom revealed in that moment was that "In the end, it's

all about Love. We are love—and meant to embody love for our Selves and be a loving presence for others. That is ultimately why we are here." This was a very powerful experience as you might imagine.

Ways to Embrace This Wisdom

Take a moment and consider how this wisdom resonates for you. Does this connect with your inner truth? Ask your Self, "how well am I able to think, show and feel Love for my Self?" On a scale of 1-10, where would you say you are now. No judgment, just bring awareness and love. What is one small action you can take to think or act in a more loving way toward your Self?

Identify several ways you are a loving presence to others in your life. Consider asking one or two loved ones how they feel and experience your love for them. Is it through words, actions, the way you look at them, the attention given? What helps you feel loving, and what are some things that get in the way of being a loving presence? Are you at times more of a worried or distracted presence?

This week, consider what opening your heart a little more to your Self and others would look like. Imagine how your life might change if you were to shift your time and attention toward Love... and like a sunflower, lean toward its light!

_____

_____

_____

_____

05
Who Do You Think
You Are!

Often, when we are doing something outside the norm, perhaps a bit bold, or proudly sharing an accomplishment, we may find our Selves on the receiving end of this critical comment. These tiny 6 words strung together can have a powerful impact on us. It is an implicit judgment that can feel shaming and accusatory, and comes from an unhealthy and fearful place within the person saying it. It may be the perfect trigger to flip on your "self-doubt" switch—making you question what you just shared, how you shared it, and if you came across as arrogant or dare I say "full of your Self." The horror!

What really would be a shame is if we let such an unkind judgment make us think twice about sharing our light, and expressing our Selves with confidence and pride. And lead us to feel or act small.

What if, instead, we hear it differently? And transform that judgment to "Yes, who do I think I am?" And allow our Selves to reflect on all the positive, kind and unique aspects of our Selves. I'll start: "I am amazing!" And "humble."☺ What about you?

Ways to Transform This Judgement

Take a moment and recognize your power in this moment. We can choose to see this unkind remark as an opportunity to reflect on the deeper question of who am I, and realize that this remark (like most) is not really about us. It is a reflection of the other person's insecurities, and unmet longings.

Bring increased awareness to how such judgments affect you. What happens to your body in those moments? Does it tighten, shrink, get hot? Where do your thoughts go? Defensive, with some reactivity? A self-doubt spiral? Or shaming and self-blaming—that I shouldn't "boast" or act proud. And what feelings arise? Sadness, fear, anger, guilt? Then give your Self much compassion.

Consider how you would have responded to someone if he/she said (or did) the same thing as you. What would a kind and loving response be? Imagine how that person would have felt after receiving your words of celebration and support for them. Now, take a moment, and say those words to your Self. How do you feel?

This week, observe if you are on the receiving end of an unkind comment, either from another person, or perhaps even your Self—through your own self-talk. Consider one way you could transform this comment, and notice the positive shift in energy and mood when you do!

_____

_____

_____

_____

06
Be Gentle With Yourself

Over the past few years, there have been extraordinary changes to our daily routines, the way we work, our social lives, our household responsibilities, and especially, our fundamental sense of safety. There has been much loss. Uncertainty has been our frequent companion, and for many—overwhelm, fear, and stress. Each of us is doing our best, with the knowledge and abilities we have, to navigate the many changes and continue moving forward.

It is during times of increased stress and uncertainty that **it is most important to be gentle with our Selves. To give to our Selves greater understanding, patience, acceptance and loving encouragement.** Acceptance of how and where we are now, and what we feel we can do each day is an act of kindness. It's counterintuitive that often the best way to move forward during times of significant stress is to slow down—our daily rhythms, our expectations of ourselves and others, and our to-do's. It is also important to tune in more deeply to what we need, what brings us peace, and lifts our spirits.

Some Ways We Can Be Gentle With Our Selves:

If we make a mistake (e.g., forget to do something), bring curiosity to it rather than judgment. If you can find any humor in it, even better! **All mistakes are really opportunities to learn more about our Selves and the situation.**

You wake up feeling tired with less energy and focus, and a long to-do list. Give your Self some extra self-care and identify the top 2-3 items from your to-do list to complete. Consider it a success if even 2 get done. Tomorrow is a new day, with likely renewed energy.

Use kind and encouraging language with your Self, and avoid fearful and critical words (e.g. "This is terrible" "I should have known," "I'm a failure"). How we talk with our Selves either lifts us up and builds confidence, or makes us feel less than.

On days of increasing anxiety, accept how you're feeling with compassion, and ask your Self what might be contributing? Then do something that grounds you and reconnects you to your center. For example, perhaps you can do a ten minute slow-breathing exercise or take a walk in nature.

This week, notice if a moment arises where you can practice being gentle with your Self. What could you do? Then go ahead and try it! It may feel uncomfortable at first. However, that's a good sign...it often means we're growing! Over time, we may start to feel more light-hearted and happy.

_____

_____

_____

_____

Self-Care: A Reflection of Self-Worth

"Self-care is an act of self-respect and self-nurturing that over time becomes a life-enhancing habit."

— DR. DANA GIONTA

07
Nourish Your Body

The word nourish means to 'feed, cherish, promote the growth of." Often, we do the first, yet do not think about cherishing or intentionally doing things which promote our body's wellbeing. Many factors get in the way, including a hectic lifestyle, stress, not liking or knowing how to cook/exercise, our environment, and the health behaviors of those closest to us. Our beliefs also play an important role. In the U.S., there's a popular belief that everyone automatically starts to have health issues, physical limitations and an expanding waist as middle-age arrives. This is fortunately not true. We can see evidence of this in other countries—and perhaps with our older friends and relatives.

There are so many things that can nourish our bodies. Just being in nature more often, and allowing the sun to shine on us for 15 minutes a day is healing and beneficial. Since being in Nevada, surrounded by natural beauty and incredible sunshine almost daily, I already can feel a noticeable difference. Spending time with positive, uplifting friends and family members who enjoy laughing and appreciate the small things in life is nourishing. Intentionally doing things which bring us joy and peace energizes us, and gives some zest to our step.☺ Practicing gratitude, eating healthy foods, and moderate size portions are other ways to care for our body.

No matter what your current health status is, by intentionally nourishing your body, you will benefit tremendously over time.

Ways to Nourish Our Body

Make time for regular self-care, no matter how busy you are. Give your Self permission to prioritize it. Experiment and see if you can increase your self-care from 25% to 35%—what would that look like? Self-care encompasses many things, including sleep, exercise, nutrition, social support, stress reduction, financial well-being, fun, and relaxation practices.

Bring increased attention to your body. How does it feel? Are there aches, stiffness, lethargy, digestive issues or a sense of vibrancy, lightness, and wellbeing? If you're experiencing any discomfort, consider getting a medical exam with comprehensive labwork (including blood and food sensitivity), and a consult with a good naturopath. Understand your current health status, and what the findings are indicating about your body's needs. Then congratulate your Self for taking this important step!

This week, reflect on the ways you are currently nourishing your body. What are they? Wonderful! Ask your Self what might help you feel more vibrant that involves your body. Perhaps your body needs more rest, or to be stretched and challenged more frequently, or healthier nutrition. Then go ahead and honor one of your body's needs, and witness the wonderful benefits that unfold.

_____

_____

_____

_____

08
Connect With Your Natural Rhythms

Many of us are disconnected from our own natural rhythms. There are many reasons for this—societal conditioning, family upbringing, educational and work cultures, the internal pressure we place on our Selves, and our beliefs.

We think that to be a good partner, parent, child, employee and friend, we need to go 24/7, in order to keep up, and do whatever is expected to be "good enough." Less frequently do we check in with our Selves and ask some important questions: "Is this really what I want to be doing?" "When is the last time I allowed my Self to rest, and enjoy just being?" "Am I allowing my Self to receive from others, or am I giving the most?" and "What am I doing for my Self that nourishes and replenishes me?"

There is a time to do, and a time to rest and renew. This is our natural human cycle. **This is how we best maintain**

our invaluable resources—our energy, our health, our positive mood, and mental attention.

Some Ways to Connect To Your Natural Rhythm

Notice how you feel when you slow down or take a break for a moment. Do feelings of guilt arise? Do any judgmental thoughts about being lazy, wasting time or not being productive enough come up? If so, this is a sign you are much more comfortable with doing than allowing your Self to just be.

The next time you feel tired or overwhelmed, give your Self permission to take a moment to rest. Ask your Self what would feel nourishing in this moment. Perhaps taking a few deep breaths, a short walk, listening to one of your favorite songs etc. Then do it, and notice how your body and energy is afterwards.

Consider setting your watch or phone to alert you 3 times each day for a week. When alerted, use this moment to connect with your Self—notice your energy level, whether you're breathing freely or holding it, how your body feels, any tension? See if you can identify any patterns.

This week, reflect on your rhythm of doing and replenishing your invaluable resources. Consider one way you can tune in further to your natural cycle. What did you discover through this deeper connection? Then take one action that supports this discovery, and watch the wonders that begin to happen!

09
Notice Your Energy

Most of us are unaware of the energy that we bring into a room, our home, or our office. We enter and often react to our environment or what's going on around us. Our energy is conveyed in many ways—through our facial expressions and body language, tone of voice, attention given, and words spoken. We don't often think about whether we are bringing positive, negative, or hyper/chaotic energy into a room.

What if others are present? How might our energy affect them?

Here are some thoughtful questions to consider:

If I bring respectful and positive energy, how might that influence others and their moods? How are these interactions likely to feel?

What will their self-esteem and sense of worth be like during and after such a positive interaction? Perhaps they will feel more valued and respected, and have greater energy.

If I bring negative energy into the room through my own stress, judgments, blaming behavior, complaining, or disrespectful language, how might this influence others and their moods?

How are they likely to feel during and after this interaction? Perhaps they will leave the room feeling small, hurt and drained. How is your energy affected after such an exchange?

We are more likely to bring negative energy into a room when we are experiencing uncomfortable feelings, self-judgment and fear.

This week, notice your energy, and if more positive, pause and appreciate your Self, and the well-being you are giving others. If negative, gently ask your Self in what ways am I possibly feeling uncomfortable, afraid, and likely judging myself? Pause, and bring curiosity and compassion to your Self in the moment. Kindness rather than judgement towards our uncomfortable feelings often works wonders!

_____

_____

_____

_____

Our Inner Compass

"Your feelings are your compass. They guide you to what's right."

— OLIVIA HAWKER

10
Honoring Our Feelings

Our feelings are often wise messengers.

However, we tend to see our feelings as either right or wrong, good or bad, positive or negative. Some we learn are acceptable to have, and others are not.

We have a feeling, and then judge it. If the judgment is negative, we then might ignore the feeling, minimize, or bury it.

We rarely just accept whatever feeling(s) arise, and let it be…with kindness. Trusting that if a feeling arose, there was a reason.

What if, instead, we were to welcome the feeling, whatever it was—sadness, anger, guilt, shame, fear, peace, joy, love, wonder.

What if our kaleidoscope of feelings were all equal in our eyes. Each one as important as the next in helping us become our true selves, and more deeply human.

What if learning to accept our feelings, all of them, as is, without judgment…set us free.

Years ago I came across a beautiful poem by Rumi about honoring our feelings. It's called **_The Guest House_**. Take a moment to read it. I think it will surprise you…it did me!

This week, consider each of your feelings as messengers—given to you each day to pay attention, and listen more closely. Are you being guided toward some action? What wonders or wisdom might you discover about You?

_____

_____

_____

_____

11
Do More of What You Love

Often we move through our lives doing the habitual things we've come to do—go to work, meet our daily responsibilities, spend time with loved ones, and perhaps some daily self-care. Some of us have hobbies that we do regularly for our well-being and social connection with others. At different times in our lives, though, we feel like we're stuck in a routine, perhaps in a rut—where one day or week feels just like the next! We may not have the energy or motivation we would like, or the enthusiasm for life that we desire.

Doing more of what you really LOVE on a daily basis is exactly what will bring you greater joy, energy and appreciation for life. It lifts our spirits, and takes us out of our routines. It also lessens the weight of our responsibilities, and allows us to feel free and joyful. We are immediately energized when we do this, and everything else in our lives feels more doable as a result.

Recently I re-connected with two things I love—dancing and relaxing by a lake. At the lake, I love reading, being in nature and watching others enjoy the fun, and carefree activities the lake offers. I also love swimming and boogie-boarding in the ocean☺ (for the beach lovers out there).

Some Wonderings about Doing More of What You Love:

Do you know some things that you LOVE to do? If so, how often do you do them? If you can't think of one thing, think about what you used to love doing, even in childhood.

If you're not often doing what you love, take a moment and ask your Self, what gets in the way? What are some things (e.g. responsibilities, beliefs, expectations) that take me away from doing the things I love and fill me with joy?

Our limiting beliefs often unconsciously prevent us from doing the things that energize us and help us feel vibrant and happy. Examples of these beliefs are: "I **should** be working during the day," "Doing something I love—before I've finished my to-do list is **irresponsible**," or "Prioritizing doing things that bring me joy is **selfish**." Observe the self-judgments in these beliefs.

What about your feelings? Notice how you feel when you consider doing something you Love. Do feelings of guilt, selfishness, or discomfort come up—either in anticipation of doing them or in the moment when you're doing them?

If so, pay close attention to these feelings, and reflect on where they might be coming from.

This week, write down some of the things you LOVE to do or used to LOVE doing—then place the list where you can see it daily. This will be a great reminder to do more of what you Love. Pick one, and plan on when, where and how you can do it this week. Give your Self 100% permission to do it. Notice how you feel while doing what you Love, afterwards, and as the week unfolds. Let the magic of doing more of what you Love begin!

_____

_____

_____

_____

12
What Nourishes You?

How rarely do we ask our Selves this question? We go about our day, our life, without really thinking about what nourishes our spirit, our heart? Often, our spirit whispers to us what it wants, what soothes and uplifts. However, for various reasons, we don't act on it. No judgment, just bring curiosity as to what gets in the way of listening, and honoring whatever comes up. Sometimes we may feel it's selfish to give to our Selves, or we're not worthy of receiving what we want. **These beliefs are unhealthy, and disconnect us from what nourishes us.**

I always knew I was moved by nature's beauty, whether it be the ocean, mountains, rainforest, sunset, etc. Even as a child, I was drawn to colors. At one point, when I was recovering from an illness, I intuitively knew being in nature for an extended period of time would be healing. And it was, much more than I ever imagined! I took a sabbatical and spent 2 months in Costa Rica. Nourishing my Self in this way led to much healing, energy, and a renewed zest for life!

Wonderings about Your Own Nourishment

Notice what brings you joy, creates a sense of inner peace, or lifts your spirit. Consider writing them down, and reflect on which ones you can bring into your life now, not one day…

Have fun, and experiment by experiencing different activities, places, cultures, people—engage all your senses—and see which ones catch your spirit's fancy. Do you feel calm, positive and energized? Those are valuable signs! **Enjoy the discovery process.**

Ask your Spirit, perhaps while on a walk, while journaling, or during a meditation/prayer, what nourishes it, and what it really wants.

What's nourishing to me? Being outdoors and surrounded by nature's beauty, vibrant colors, music that moves me, journaling, reading something inspirational, travel and experiencing new cultures, good conversations, and laughter with friends. What about You?

This week, select one of the above exercises and pay attention to what is nourishing to your Spirit. Then reflect on how you can integrate 1-2 of these discoveries into the weeks ahead, and watch the wonder that unfolds!

_____

_____

_____

_____

13
Make Time for Peace

Often we find our Selves pulled in many directions, overwhelmed with daily obligations and an endless to-do list, and unsettled by what is happening in our world. Many of us try to cope by doing more each day or doing things faster or more efficiently. Some days we "succeed" better than others. However, often there is a cost over time on our well-being and our relationships.

How might you feel if each day you were to ask your Self, what would bring me peace…in this moment, in this day? Could taking time to pause, and allowing your Self a few deep, relaxing breaths bring a moment of peace? Try a simple exercise: **Breathe in through your nose (a normal breath in) and out through your mouth, as if you are blowing out candles (exhale to the count of 4).** That's it! Aim for 1 minute, and notice how you feel afterwards. Build up to 3 minutes.

Here are some other ways to create moments of peace:

Give yourself 5 minutes and reflect on what you are grateful for in your life right now. Then let yourself feel the abundance of your blessings.

Take a 15 minute walk outdoors, and let the beauty of nature work its magic.

Sit by a lake or the ocean for 20-30 minutes and let your Self just be. Enjoy the feeling of peace that comes. This is one of my favorite ways to feel at peace.

Let your senses bring you **into the present, where peace is most easily experienced.** Take about 3 minutes and connect with each sense—sight, sound, touch, taste and smell—wherever you are.

*Add the breathing exercise discussed to any of the above, and you have a wonderful double dose of peace!☺

A Reflective Pause

At this point, it's been approximately three months since you've begun reading *52 Weeks to Self-Love*. There's been new concepts and action steps taken, and likely valuable insights, and Self-discoveries along the way.

I've found it very helpful to Pause at different moments in my life, so I'd like to invite you to also pause and:

Reflect on the last few months, and consider the following:

1. What concepts have you found the most helpful so far, and why?

   _____

   _____

   _____

2. Which 1-3 practices have you integrated into your daily/weekly routine and how have they been helpful?

   _____

   _____

   _____

3. In what ways have you stretched your Self, and taken some uncomfortable and even courageous action steps?

_____

_____

_____

4. Share 2-3 new insights and Self-discoveries you've had along the way.

_____

_____

_____

Celebrate your Self for taking this time to reflect, for the courageous steps you've taken so far, and the small and larger ways you've grown over the past few months.

Fear

"The purpose of life is to live it, to taste experience to the utmost, to reach out eagerly and without fear for newer and richer experience"

— ELEANOR ROOSEVELT

14
Make Friends With Fear

Often, when fear arises in us, we do various things to cope with it—avoid, minimize, deny, judge, placate, get angry, or engage in one of many less than healthy habits. This is because fear, like several other emotions we may label as "negative" is uncomfortable. Because we are uncomfortable feeling discomfort, we go into our familiar toolbox and rely on one of our trusted and familiar strategies to deal with this uninvited guest. Usually this is a strategy we've learned in our childhood or young adulthood. By doing this, however, we often then do not deal with the cause of the fear. Many times, the catalyst of the fear is growth—doing something that is outside our comfort zone. And by taking action, stretching our Selves, we build confidence!

Many of us put off dreams we've had for years, and avoid making a change we know is important, because of fear.

What if, instead, we decide to get more comfortable with our discomfort and begin building a positive relationship with our "negative" emotions, such as fear. We could do this with anger, sadness, shame, jealousy, and helplessness also. Instead of going into our safety toolbox, we can choose to bring curiosity to our fear—with the desire to get to know it better. We can do this by gently asking it—Fear—direct questions, such as, "What is it that is making you feel afraid?," "What do you need in this moment that would help you feel safe?," "Where in my body do you, Fear, like to show up?," "What are you trying to protect me from?," and "If I do X, what would that mean for you?"

As you ask these questions, pause and take several deep breaths between each. Then listen closely to what Fear shares with you. Consider thanking it for trusting you enough to open up, like you would a friend who allowed herself to be vulnerable with you. By listening with kindness, without judgment, you build trust.

This week, notice any sensations of fear that may show up. Consider sitting with Fear for one minute, just noticing your thoughts, any judgments you have about Fear showing up uninvited, and sensations in your body. Then, kindly ask Fear several questions, either from above or your own. Pause between and take several breaths. Let it know it's safe to share with you. Listen carefully... what does it tell you?

_____

_____

_____

_____

15
Fear is the Start of Courage

Many times we think less of our Selves because we feel afraid. Fear may arise when we think of doing something for the first time. It often surfaces when we attempt an action that doesn't seem part of our self-concept, or is outside our comfort zone. Fear often appears when we have a strong desire or dream to do something that means a great deal to us... and the risk of failure feels too painful. The wonder of this is that it is universal. It is a reflection of our being human. **Experiencing fear does not make us less than... in any way.**

What if we were to think of fear as the seed of Courage blossoming within us. One cannot have courage without fear. Being courageous is moving forward with fear—ever present. Some moments, it may feel like fear is walking beside you as you take steps. Other moments it's in front—making it very difficult to move at all toward the life changes you desire.

Know that this experience of fear is a good sign. It means you desire to grow, move beyond your comfort zone, and care about whatever is bringing up the fear. When this happens, let yourself BE with it. Resist the reflex (and conditioned habit) to push it or should it away. Trust that courage is beginning to blossom within you, as you nurture this desire or new endeavor. Remember imperfect action—and that perfectionism has no place on our learning curve.

Embracing fear as the first step on the path of Courage:

Allow your Self to feel the fear, without judgment.

Be with the fear for a few moments. Notice what thoughts arise. Ask your Self, what is the worst that could happen if I take action toward this endeavor?

Breathe in through your nose and out through your mouth for 3-5 minutes. Let your Self get more acquainted with the fear, as you imagine the worst scenarios.

Now, imagine what is the best outcome that may happen? How might You and your life change by moving forward—with fear by your side? Notice the feelings that arise as you reflect on this.

A wonderful acronym that I came across for FEAR is Face Everything and Rise.

This week, consider something you've desired to do (or try for the first time), and have been afraid to start. Identify what that first small step might be. Let your Self feel the fear, as you imagine taking that first step.

And, if you're feeling fearfully courageous, go ahead and take that step! See what amazing things begin to unfold as your Courage and confidence grows.

_____

_____

_____

_____

16
The Courage to Have Difficult Conversations

hroughout our lives, there will be moments that require courage. Courage, not avoidance behavior, however tempting that may feel to do in the moment. Often, someone may say or do something, likely unintentionally, that may hurt, disappoint or anger us. Perhaps they've crossed one of our boundaries—such as treating us disrespectfully, or not showing up for something very important to us with no explanation.

We have an important choice in these moments.

To say something, and give this person an opportunity (and the benefit of the doubt) to understand how his/her actions affected us, and amend the situation. Through this, we can hopefully heal what happened, build trust through the heartfelt conversation, and strengthen the relationship. Many times the situation is a result of misperceptions or misunderstandings. Unfortunately, the more common response is to say nothing or complain to another person about the situation.

However, saying nothing rarely works because inadvertently we are communicating to them. Our hurt or angry feelings are showing up in the relationship as withdrawal, tension, shutting down—or leaking out as frustration, a short fuse, tearfulness, reduced interest, or resentment. Over time, this begins to negatively affect our trust and sense of safety, both of which are pillars for a healthy and positive relationship.

Ways To Find Your Courage

Ask your Self how important this person or relationship is to you. If not important, then you can consider letting it go, or distancing your Self by spending less time with him/her. However, if this relationship is important, and you feeling strongly about what happened, or there is a pattern to the behavior, then courage is required.

Consider first speaking with a trusted friend, therapist, or coach about the situation, if having a direct conversation with this person feels difficult or anxiety-provoking. You can process your feelings with this trusted person, and role-play different ways/language you could use to communicate directly with the person you are having difficulty with.

Identify 5 different alternate perceptions or reasons for why this situation might have happened. Use your imagination. Do any of these additional perceptions expand your feelings of empathy or compassion for your Self or the other person? Ask your Self, "What am I afraid will happen—if I were to speak directly with this person about my feelings and thoughts about his/her behavior?"

The best way to build courage is through action.

This week, reflect on a situation that would benefit from being addressed directly. Notice any area in your life where you feel frustration or resentment—these are helpful clues. Consider what would most help you connect to your courage, and have a direct conversation with the person about whatever situation is on your mind.

Then act courageously (even if you don't feel it) and do it! Be open to the gifts that come from honoring your Self in this way, and the relationship.

_____

_____

_____

_____

The Landscape of Your Mind

"Your Mind will pull you in a thousand different directions at once, but your Soul knows the Way.
Just breath, just be.
Return to who you really are."

— AFFINITY SOUL

17
What Are You
Believing?

We are often aware of what is happening around us—in our homes, neighborhoods, workplaces, and country. However, many of us are much less aware of what is happening in the inner world of our mind. This inner mind is rich with thoughts, beliefs, feelings, and images that influence our behaviors and the life choices we make. It also create our limits—what we believe is possible or impossible for our Selves and our future. A powerful way to change our life and future opportunities is to change our current beliefs, which are often limiting.

Our beliefs are our deeply entrenched thoughts that frequently lie at the outer rim of our consciousness. These might include our beliefs around money, health, success, people, and worldly topics. We are generally aware of our beliefs around religion/spirituality, politics, gay rights, right and wrong, and "good" parenting. However, we are often less aware of the beliefs we have about our Selves.

What if we became more conscious of the beliefs we have about our Selves—**our abilities, talents, intelligence, appearance, personality, inner strength(s), and potential.**

Clarifying Our Beliefs:

Take 5-10 minutes, and choose several areas about your Self, outlined above. Then ask your Self, "What do I believe about my talents and ability to learn?" Or, "What are my beliefs about my intelligence or my ability to manage money?" Then do a freestyle exercise by writing your response to each question without stopping for 2-3 minutes.

Reflect on your responses, and notice any pattern to your Self beliefs. Are they more positive or negative in general, or varied? Do they feel limiting or more expansive, reflecting possibility? If limiting, consider which experiences or influences may have contributed to those beliefs.

If you'd like more clarity about your Self beliefs in these areas, or found the exercise challenging, you can ask a close friend or trusted family member to help. Ask what he/she thinks are some of the key beliefs you have about your Self, and if they've noticed any limiting beliefs you may have. This takes some courage, but the rewards are worth it!

This week, reflect on what you discovered about your Self and your beliefs. Choose one belief you'd like to makeover, so it can enhance your sense of Self and the possibilities you see for your life.

Bring loving-kindness to that old belief, and replace it with a healthier belief that supports you and the future you desire. Repeat this new belief often and watch the wonders that unfold!

_____

_____

_____

_____

18
Shift Your Perspective

I n this moment in time, there are many diverse stressors—the economy, political uncertainty, societal unrest,
and ongoing environmental challenges that can lead
us to perceiving our life and the world with gray colored
glasses. It is often easier to focus on what is problematic
or causing us distress, as our minds attach more readily
to negative emotional stimuli. When we do this, we are
limiting our vision and only seeing part of our reality. This
often leads us to feeling down, stressed, or less than by only
seeing what's not working or what we don't have.

What if, instead, we thought of this as a habit that is no
longer serving us. **And decide to shift towards seeing our
reality with a more balanced, truer perspective.**

Some Ways We Can Shift
Our Perspective:

Let's bring increased attention to our thoughts, and notice
when we are having a negative perspective about a person/

situation. First, identify the negative perspective. Then let's **shift to the "realm of possibility" (ROP)** and ask ourselves, "What is a more neutral interpretation of this?" For example, "This situation could go either way, there's no way to accurately predict the future." And, how might we possibly think about this same situation in a positive way?

Each time we find ourselves thinking negatively, let's practice the "realm of possibility" thinking—by also holding in our mind a neutral and then positive perspective as well. Observe the calm that begins to happen when you do this ROP practice.

Take a moment and think about all the people, gifts, and experiences you have in your life now that you are grateful for. Perhaps it is your health and the health of your loved ones. Or the advanced technology that enables you to stay connected with those you love. As you reflect on what you're grateful for, the deeper benefits come by letting your Self really feel the joy, wonder, and peace of such blessings in your life. A gift of gratitude is that it can shift our perspective in that moment! It doesn't require doing it regularly to receive positive benefits.

Give your mind and body a rest, and re-center your Self through a short 10-minute meditation. As we feel calmer, our perspective will often naturally shift, without even trying. How helpful is that!

If you are feeling down, overwhelmed, or being judgmental towards your Self or others, pause and imagine what a wise and caring friend would say to you about this situation.

This week, decide which of the suggestions above you'd like to try, and when you feel like your perspective needs a lift, do it! If you can try it several times over the week, even better. And notice any shifts in your mood and energy as well.

_____

_____

_____

_____

19
Flip the Switch

Often, something happens and we get "triggered." Meaning, we experience some type of emotional response to a person or situation, and a particular thought switch goes on. We may have multiple thought switches, however, usually we have our top 2-3 favorites.☺ One switch could be "what did I do wrong?…what's wrong with me?…and why does this keep happening?" Another could be "How could I say something so foolish…What was I thinking…I'm always putting my foot in my mouth." Lastly, because three's a charm "I wasn't invited…I thought they liked me….I never fit in."

We can think of it as a flipped switch. Once flipped, a particular current of thoughts starts, depending on the situation. **We all have these switches—part of being our vulnerable, imperfect, human Selves.** As you've noticed, these switches often have more of a negative slant. This often leads to us feeling bad about our Selves and some-how less than.

Ways to Flip the Switch

Reflect on your top two or three switches that most often get flipped by some situation. Notice if there's a common theme among them, or if there's a unique emotion connected to each. Possible themes can be not feeling appreciated, not feeling good enough, or not belonging or fitting in—all of which lead to the experience of not feeling loved.

Select the one that has the least emotional impact and begin noticing each time it gets turned on. What types of situation(s) or interactions 'switch' it on? If you could give this switch a name, what would you call it? **For example, it could be the "I'm a big failure" switch.**

Decide how you can flip off (oops)—just flip the switch, and instead give your Self grace and compassion in that moment of humanness. What would that look like? Ask your Self how this situation could be seen in a more neutral or positive light? Is it possible that this incident may be more about the other person than you?

This week, identify one of your switches and notice how you feel and react when it gets flipped. What is one small way you can bring more kindness to your Self in that moment?

How might the current of thoughts change if you were giving your Self the love and compassion you desired? Go ahead, and try it! Notice the increasing sense of peace you begin to feel.

_____

_____

_____

_____

20
Is It Really Impossible?

O ften, our goals and dreams may feel out of our reach or perhaps even impossible.

This is the 10th year of my journey toward vibrant health. With much gratitude, I'm getting very close! It has, like many things in life, been a winding trail—with detours, bumps, frightening moments, discouragement, tears, failures and… wonder, joy, excitement, relief, renewed hope, perseverance, determination and courage.

At the time, I didn't believe some of the health changes were possible, like losing more than 5 lbs—since I had tried unsuccessfully for years! I never would have believed that I could lose 35 lbs, and be the lightest I've been in 30 years. I thought this was truly impossible—far beyond what I could have imagined for my Self. Experiencing that this was indeed possible has been an invaluable and life-changing lesson for me.

To get to this place of renewed health, I had to make major changes—to my lifestyle, way of eating, mindset, self-care practices, and relationships. I also began researching and opening to alternative approaches to healing. Most of these took courage...more than I realized in those moments. Only when I look back do I see how courageous many of those changes were. **They required me to get out of my comfort zone and let go of conditioned ways of thinking.** One of the many health changes I made was to significantly reduce sugar in my life. I then started to eliminate gluten & dairy. I'm not fully there yet!

I am coming to believe that living our lives more vibrantly involves cultivating courage, developing a kind relationship with Fear, and making some courageous changes. With such changes comes greater confidence—an unexpected and beautiful gift!

Ways to Move Toward The "Impossible"

What goals and dreams do you have that you've been afraid to move toward, perhaps tried but not succeeded, or have no idea how to begin? Ask your Self, "How long have I been wanting to do or have this? And, "How important is this to me?" Reflect on why this is important to you and how your life would be different if you were to reach your goal or start moving toward your dream, whatever that may be.

Consider if there is a hidden belief you may have that whatever you most hope for is impossible? Take 3 minutes on your own, without distraction, and imagine actually reaching that goal or dream. Notice what feelings and thoughts arise as you do. Were they mostly positive—or did self-doubt, fear, and more negative thinking arise? If negative, just bring curiosity and compassion to them.

This week, identify one goal or dream you have that is important to you, and that you would feel excited and happy to ultimately reach! What is it? Consider one small action step you could take that feels like a positive start.

Remember, it is action that creates motivation—and I dare say, inspiration! Perhaps it is reaching out for support (from a friend, co-worker, or coach) or talking with others who have been successful in achieving a similar goal or dream.

_____

_____

_____

On Living Consciously

"I am who I am today because of the choices I made yesterday."

— ELEANOR ROOSEVELT

21
The Nonlinear Nature of Progress

Often, we have an unconscious schema in our minds that we use to evaluate our progress. It typically involves hard work, hours versus minutes of engagement, and feeling like it's effortful rather than done with ease. And there's also a quantity of some sort that is involved (eg. 6 items on a checklist). If any one of these are not met, we come away concluding that we failed or barely made progress. Or perhaps even worse, that We are failures.

An example of this occurred with my coaching client who is quite accomplished and is contracted with a publisher to write a book—a life dream of hers! She matter of factly declared that the 25,000 words she had written over the summer didn't count at all. And that she was a failure on some level.

She believed this because how she wrote it went against the schema above. Instead of sitting for hours and feeling like she was struggling to write—she wrote it while dictating it on her morning nature walk, or during 15 minutes of inspiration while dealing with summer chores and family responsibilities. It felt easy and natural overall, with moments of deep fulfillment and even joy. We explored her limiting narrative and after a few sessions, she had a wonderful breakthrough, and is confidently on her way to completing her first draft. She now feels excitement rather than anxiety and failure when thinking about her book and progress overall.

I reflected on where this schema originated, and on how deeply woven it is into our concept of work and progress. Who said that our work has to feel hard, and that it requires us to focus on it for hours at a time—rather than in shorter increments? And that it needs to happen at a desk or office, rather than while waiting in a car, at a cafe, or even on a walk at the beach. Extra-ordinary things happen when our brain gets to rest!

Some Ways to Embrace Nonlinear Progress:

Notice how you currently work—and if you also have a schema with any of the above factors influencing you. Then bring increased attention to any judgements you may have as to what the "correct" way or environment is for working.

Give your Self permission to release those judgements and see what positive shifts may come.

Imagine the possibility of progress happening with ease, a side-step or two and even some joy. Where are you now, on a scale of 1-10 (10 much ease) related to your work? What would it look like if you went from a 5 to a 6 over the next few weeks?

This week, consider conducting a fun experiment and let your Self do some of your work or related projects in short increments and/or in inspired spurts. How does it feel to be engaged for shorter periods and when you feel inspired? What are some of the results? I wouldn't be surprised if you experience some impressive momentum this way!

_____

_____

_____

_____

22
Our Relationship with Time

Often, we feel we must use our time wisely. Be productive. Do something that moves our Selves or life forward to a more positive future state. We keep a future Self in mind who would then benefit from our present "valuable" use of our time. This can lead to pressure to be productive with our time and not "waste it" by doing nothing. Implicit in this is an underlying state of striving, and expectations for our relationship with Time.

What are the expectations we might have? Is it that we must always be **doing** something with it? And that doing must be something that feels useful or that others' deem productive? That what I'm doing today will lead to xyz tomorrow? There is a place for this way of thinking and approach to how we use our time.

I wonder though how this affects our ability to just Be with Time. To allow our Selves the freedom and spaciousness to just Be with whatever leisure time we may have, without any pressure or guilt to Do anything. To be on the "receiving end" of whatever may unfold in that hour or two without needing to do anything to "justify one's existence." How wonderful, yes! This quote is from an excellent book, *Four Thousand Weeks, Time Management for Mortals* by Oliver Burkeman. He talks about the instrumentalization of Time, and how our relationship with Time evolved into that of doing—with an emphasis on productivity with a future state in mind. I highly recommend it if any of the above resonates with you.

Ways to Be and Embrace the Gift of Leisure:

Bring increased attention to a typical day of yours. Of the 16-18 hours awake, how much of this time is set aside to relax, enjoy, and renew? Notice the feelings which may arise with any down time? Is there any anxiety, guilt, niggling sense that you "should" do something productive with this time? Allow your Self to feel this, then take three calming breaths in and out—releasing any pressure you're feeling in that moment.

Imagine 30 minutes of pure uninterrupted, leisure time to just Be, with no guilt or should's. You have my 100% permission.☺ What might that look like for you? Release any thoughts about Doing something with it. Reflect on allowing your Self to just be. Might you take a siesta, sip a comforting cup of tea, journal in a lovely book, sit outside and observe nature? One of the gifts where I live now are the beautiful hummingbirds I get to see daily. It brings me real joy taking a moment to watch them.

This week, reflect on your current relationship with Time. Is it a friendly one or more adversarial, feeling like you're always fighting with it, being rushed, and pushed around by it? Consider how you might create a more positive and gentler relationship with it.

Identify one small step you can take this week to relax the grip of pressure, shoulds, future strivings—and enjoy the moment, allowing it to Be just as it is. This likely will feel uncomfortable at first. However, what a beautiful gift this becomes over time... if we let it!

_____

_____

_____

_____

23
A Path to Success

Too often, when we start working toward a goal or pursuing a dream, we unconsciously think we need to do it alone. Just imagining our Selves taking on a goal that feels daunting, or a dream that seems almost impossible on our own is enough to stop many from even taking the first step! I know this to be true because I've been there, a number of times in my life. There are many reasons for this—lack of know how if it's the first time doing, overwhelm of where to start, well-meaning loved ones telling us it's a "crazy" idea, "likely to fail," or "not responsible." Additionally, we often have our own fears and self-doubts about doing, and receiving such feedback can magnify exponentially such feelings.

What I've discovered after much trial and error, and reflecting on my successes (and failures) is that the single greatest factor that's helped me make courageous changes in my life that felt very scary at the time, and accomplish what I have to date is Not doing it alone. This can take different forms.

An example of this was when I began feeling burnout at work in 2014, as well as some health issues, and intuitively knew I needed to pause. I wanted to take a sabbatical of at least 2 months—yet I was afraid if I closed my therapy and coaching business for that extent of time, I would have no business to return to.

I decided to hire a coach, the first time in my life, to help me process the many uncomfortable feelings that were arising, as well as the fearful and limiting thoughts and beliefs. Having the courage and vulnerability to reach out was invaluable. Spending 2 months in Costa Rica by the water was exactly what I needed to heal and renew. I returned with much energy and renewed joy and appreciation for my work and clients—many of whom chose to wait!

Another example is writing my first book, "*From Stressed to Centered: A Practical Guide to a Healthier and Happier You.*" I very likely would not have written it if I hadn't reached out to a colleague and shared my idea of cowriting a book together on stress and self-care, given our similar areas of expertise. He loved the idea, and the book was "birthed" in our imagination. Actually Doing it, however, took much effort, a significant learning curve into the publishing world, and overcoming many obstacles—including our own internal fears and self-doubts about sharing our voices, stories, and expertise with the world.

Ways toward Your Path to Success:

What goals and dreams do you have for your Self now? IF you haven't yet paused to reflect on this, give yourself this gift, and do so in the next two weeks. Write them down and make them visible for you to see daily. Your future Self will be very grateful to present You for doing so.

Consider making a list and writing down the top 5-7 things getting in the way of you moving forward with whatever goal/dream you've identified above. Afterwards, identify how Not doing it alone and reaching out for what you need—support, a mindset shift, accountability, knowledge—on 1 of the items on your list can be the catalyst to taking the first courageous step toward your heart's desire. Which item did you choose?

This week, reflect on the best action step you can take that will feel empowering, perhaps even exciting, towards realizing a path to your success, however You define it—which embraces Not doing it alone. What does that look like?

And just imagine how Good it will feel to take that step with greater confidence! As my exchange daughter Lorenza often says "You can Do it!" I wholeheartedly agree!!

_____

_____

_____

_____

24
Celebrate

The Latin etymology of celebrate means "assemble to honor or acknowledge." I love that honoring is part of what celebration means. How often do we honor our Selves, and acknowledge not only what we do, but who we are—our values, character, strengths and dreams? Most of us are busy trying to meet our responsibilities and complete our to-do lists that we often shift from one goal or accomplishment to the next. We rarely pause to acknowledge the time, energy, skill and commitment that led to our successes. Even less do we acknowledge the incremental steps of progress and hurdles overcome that directly led to our successes, large and small.

We don't celebrate for many reasons. Besides busyness, we may feel undeserving, guilty or believe "who do I think I am" to celebrate. Perhaps we have a hard time even seeing our strengths and successes, making it difficult then to acknowledge them, and almost impossible to celebrate.

What if we consider celebrating as a wonderful habit we haven't yet developed? As we practice celebrating our Selves and our accomplishments—one incremental step forward at a time—we give ourselves the gift of acknowledgement. We can also celebrate others in our lives, their uniqueness, beauty and accomplishments. Taking time to **see** our Selves and others provides a fertile soil for us to blossom.

Cultivating the Habit of Celebrating

Identify one goal you have now. Clarify the incremental steps and estimated time frame needed to reach this goal. As you reach each step, take time to acknowledge your positive momentum and this mini-success. How might you acknowledge your Self so that if feels like a celebration, an honoring in some way?

Consider keeping a celebration journal, reflecting each day on 1-2 things you would like to honor and give attention to. For example, it could be about your unique qualities and strengths; a habit or skill you're developing; or progress made toward a goal.

Join a group of like-minded people or have get-togethers with friends who also would like to develop a celebration practice. This is an opportunity to share with each other things over the past month about your Self you would like to celebrate, and also something about one another you can honor. Let your Self get creative and have fun with this!

This week, select one of the above celebration practices you would like to try. Which one speaks to your heart, and feels good? Start with that, and if it feels uncomfortable or awkward at first, that's normal. As you continue to do, notice any shifts in your feelings, mood, or confidence? Perhaps a bit lighter and happier! And any wonderful shifts in those you've gathered together to celebrate?

_____

_____

_____

_____

Prioritize
Your Happiness

"It's not selfish to love your Self, take care of
your Self, and to make your happiness a priority.
It is essential."

— MANDY HALE

25
The Life You've
Imagined for Yourself

One of the biggest regrets people have as they are dying is that they didn't live the life they wanted. They often did what others expected of them, putting family, friends' and everyone else's needs above their own. Many of us learn in childhood and through various life roles to put our needs last. We may have strong desires, however, we don't feel worthy enough to truly have what we want, so we don't try.

Many of us also feel guilty if we do consider our own needs in addition to others'. This guilt contributes to us not setting boundaries in our relationships when our intuition and body are loudly signaling we need to. Maybe we were called selfish when we did try to care for our Selves. Perhaps we don't feel strong enough to cope if we go for it, and don't succeed. How disappointing that may be. Where would that leave us? Experiencing these uncomfortable and painful feelings can lead us over time to unintentionally disconnect from our deepest needs and desires—as a way to protect our Selves.

Often, we have a niggling sense, a quiet voice whispering to us that this isn't the life we imagined for our Selves. That "I'm not living my own life." The life that I really want—whether that's traveling around the world, becoming an artist, finally getting that college degree, starting our own business, or having a child. Sometimes it presents itself through an area of our lives that brings repeated frustration and disappointment. It's important to pay attention to this quiet voice—our intuitive sense—that we are not living true to our Selves.

Considerations on Living The Life You've Imagined:

Reflect on how well you know your Self, what are your important needs? Write them down, and ask your Self, "How well am I meeting my own needs, as well as others'?" If there is an imbalance, notice this. Identify one action you can take to rebalance this, and better prioritize your own needs.

What are 3-5 deep desires you have? Are several of these a part of the life you've imagined for your Self? If so, pause and realize that these desires of yours merit your time and attention. With intention, take courageous action toward realizing them.

If you're finding it difficult to take a step toward this, identify one to two obstacles you feel are blocking your ability to do so. Is there a healthy boundary you want to set, but are afraid of hurting someone if you do? Are there societal values / dictates of what success is that feel confusing and distracting you from what your heart wants? Perhaps you have limiting beliefs that what you really want isn't possible for you.

This week, identify one action you can take that would feel aligned with the life you've imagined for your Self. It could be anything—a small step or a leap—in the direction of your desired life!

_____

_____

_____

_____

26
The Way of The
Sunflower

Sunflowers are one of my favorite flowers, which we are seeing everywhere with the arrival of fall. I find them so cheerful, love the bright yellow colors, and the incredible height and strength of them. Seeing fields of sunflowers when visiting the Provence region of France five years ago brought me immense joy. One of the characteristics I love most about the sunflowers is how they turn naturally toward the light. This process supports their impressive growth and vitality.

Many times, we too may instinctively feel like turning toward the light. As humans, that can be something that brings us joy and peace, and lifts our spirits. However, we often stop our Selves with feelings of guilt or selfishness if we "indulge" in activities or moments that bring us joy. Thoughts like "I don't have time to do that," "I should be doing x," "This isn't responsible," "This is silly," and "It's the middle of the day" get in the way, and block us from turning naturally toward our light.

Why is this so important? Because we as the beautiful, vulnerable humans that we are, like the sunflower, can only continue to grow and thrive when we allow our Selves to embrace what gives us light. Engaging in what nourishes our body, spirit and minds, and brings us joy and peace **regularly,** is essential for us to blossom fully.

The Way of the Sunflower

Consider what embracing the way of the sunflower might look like for you? What activities, little things, experiences or daily rituals feel like sunshine to you? Specifically, what brings you joy, peace, and feels nourishing to you? Take a moment and write them down.

Reflect on how often you are engaging in them now on a daily or weekly basis? If unclear, consider keeping a log for a week and recording what brings you joy, energy and nourishment each day. Notice what feelings and thoughts come up as you consider doing this log exercise. And what arises for you when you're thinking about turning toward the light? Are there any feelings or thoughts that feel like clouds getting in the way?

This week, consider placing what you've identified as the activities, moments, rituals, etc. that bring you joy and feel like sunshine in a visible location in your home. Then select one activity from this list, and give your Self permission to be like the sunflowers and turn toward the light.

As you do something each day, notice the ripples of joy and a lightness in your step as the week goes on.

_____

_____

_____

_____

27
Nurture Your Desires

Often when we think about our desires, conflicting thoughts and feelings arise. We may want to pursue them, but limiting thoughts can get in the way. For example, "It's impossible," "It would take years," or perhaps "I have no idea where to start." Feelings of fear, guilt, or anxiety may arise. It can have the quality of being more like a dream, than a heartfelt desire.

I recently looked up the etymology of the word "desire," which I loved. It comes from the phrase **de sidere**, which means **"from the stars…awaiting what the stars will bring."** When we have a desire, it can linger with us over months or even years…often receding into the background of our minds. Then elicited by a specific moment, it reappears into our consciousness and touches our hearts once again. **This is a cue that this Desire is coming from a deep place within us, and is worthy of our attention.** It is likely coming from your heart and spirit, and perhaps it is also coming from the stars…another beautiful mystery of life!

The rhythms of our lives have a way of disconnecting us from what is important to us, if we let them. By making time to reflect on our heartfelt desires, we are not only "awaiting for the stars to bring them," but are nurturing them with intention. This process helps us stay connected to what is truly important to us and allows us to first hear our heart's longing and then courageously move toward it.

Some Ways We Can Nurture Our Desires:

Imagine this desire is truly possible. What would that look like? How might you and your life change if your heartfelt desire appeared…like a beautiful long–awaited guest.

Foster your belief that your desire can be achieved. Spend time each week daydreaming about your desire, and notice how you feel before and after. Do you feel more excited about your life?

Journal weekly about a longing you have, and explore how you can begin to nurture it consistently. Perhaps you can create a visual daily reminder in your home or office, bringing attention to your desire each day.

Consider joining a group of like-minded people with similar desires. This will give you an opportunity to share stories and resources, and to encourage one another to continue nurturing your desire by taking little steps.

This week, reflect on one heartfelt desire you have that you believe would really bring you joy, and make your life feel vibrant. The size of the desire is not important. Ask your Self, what has kept me from taking steps toward my Desire, and listening to my heart? Then identify one small step you can take this week towards this "gift from the stars."

_____

_____

_____

_____

28
Find Your Joy Each Day

Life has a tendency to go by very quickly, especially as we get older. We often feel as if we never have enough time to do the things we want, or complete everything on our to do list. Because of this, we put off doing favorite hobbies, pursuing passions, "indulging" in self-care, and fun leisure activities until later…when we have more time. The problem is that time rarely comes, as something else fills the space. Another obligation, responsibility, or appointment gets our attention.

Unfortunately taking care of all of these tasks week after week, without making time for activities that bring us joy, lift our spirits and renew our minds/bodies, often lead us to feeling weighed down and unhappy.

What if we were to begin prioritizing joy each day. Yes, you heard me, **each day**, not once a week or something we save for the weekends! What we prioritize, and therefore give our attention to, often gets done. Imagine how you might feel at the end of your week if each day you experienced some joy. How would your mood, energy, and body likely feel after experiencing joy over weeks and months?

Ways We Can Find Joy Each Day:

Start by giving your Self permission to experience joy, despite whatever difficulties and hardship is going on around us. There is extraordinary stress and uncertainty currently in the world, which can make it more challenging for us to do this.

Many of us also have the unconscious belief that prioritizing joy is indulgent, selfish, and not responsible. It often makes us feel uncomfortable to make joy more central in our daily lives. **Doing it may begin to feel so good that we then experience guilt for feeling happier in our lives. Or perhaps afraid that it won't last.**

The incredible and surprising benefit of finding joy each day is that it often gives us more energy, and increases our motivation and zest for living. We then find ourselves getting more done, and managing our responsibilities with greater ease and less effort. How wonderful and wise is that!

This week, conduct a joy experiment. Ask your Self, what would bring me joy today? It could be anything...listening to your favorite music, talking to a friend, baking a special dish, spending time with loved ones, or engaging in a passion/hobby at some point during the day. Ask the question, and pay close attention to whatever comes to mind (even if it sounds odd). Then do your best to do it! Notice the positive energy and mood lifts that come.

_____

_____

_____

_____

A Reflective Pause

Over the past 3 months, there's been new concepts, practices, action steps taken and likely valuable insights, and Self-discoveries along the way.

I've found it very helpful to Pause at different moments in my life, so I'd like to invite you to also pause and:

Reflect on the last few months, and consider the following:

1. What concepts have you found most helpful so far? And why?

   _____

   _____

   _____

2. Which 2-3 practices have you integrated into your daily or weekly routine, and how have they been helpful?

   _____

   _____

   _____

3. In what ways have you stretched your Self, and taken some courageous action steps?

_____

_____

_____

4. Share 2-3 of your favorite insights and the Self-discoveries you've had along the way.

_____

_____

_____

Celebrate your Self for taking this time to reflect, for all the courageous steps you've taken so far… and the small and larger ways you've blossomed over the past few months

Holidays

"One of the most important ways to reduce stress is to ask for help. This works not only during the holidays, but also all year round."

— Dr. Daisy Sutherland

29
Gifts of Gratitude for Thanksgiving (and other Holidays)

As the Thanksgiving holiday closely approaches, let us remember to:

Be gentle with our Selves. We are all doing the best we can. ♡

Give our Selves permission to rest, and take some time for ourselves. It will allow the best version of our Selves to show up, and be present.

Set a healthy boundary with family members, friends and others—and honor our own needs, instead of always putting others' needs above ours.

Let our Selves experience Joy without an ounce of guilt. Life is short, and each holiday with loved ones is a gift.

Be open to Receiving the unique blessings this Thanksgiving might bring...whatever that may be for you.

And reflect on all You have to be grateful for—our Gratitudes I like to say—in our Lives at this time. By focusing on what is going well and what we have—rather than what we wish we had (or don't have), we lay the foundation to experience greater joy, peace and abundance in our Lives.

This week, consider three things you are grateful for in your life at this time, and identify one way you will give your Self some Love and self-care during this extra busy time.

_____

_____

_____

_____

30
Uninvited Guest At Our Door

The holidays are often a time of joy, cheer and uplifting moments and moods. They take us out of our normal routines, and give us the opportunity to show others how much we love and care about them. This can be through gifts and more deeply, through acts of kindness and giving. Sometimes, however, unexpected events—such as deaths, illnesses, accidents and more predictable experiences, like the anniversaries of loved ones deaths or previous hurtful memories around the holidays show up. Often, we don't want to experience sadness, grief and perhaps anger or traumatic memories during a time of year that's supposed to be happy. Yet…we do. Our lives are frequently a mix of yin and yang.

Over the past several weeks, I learned of the somewhat unexpected death of a close friend's husband who I knew well, the very unexpected death of my neighbor's 26 y.o. son who I've come to know in Vegas, and had somewhat of a health scare myself. First shock and disbelief, then my old friend Grief arrived. Our feelings such as grief, fear and anger are like uninvited guests that arrive at our doorstep. What do we typically do when they knock? Do we ignore them and pretend we didn't hear the knock, put headphones on to avoid it, tell them to go away, they're not welcome here; or do we run out the back door.☺ Less frequently do we open the door and kindly (and sometimes, bravely) invite them in. So we can get to know each of them, and perhaps befriend them over time. All of our feelings serve a valuable purpose in our lives. And they are invaluable guides to what is healthy and right for us…

There's a beautiful poem called the Guest House by Rumi, which I often share with my clients. It invites us to practice a welcoming and loving relationship with our feelings. I recommend you read it several times over the course of a month to let the depth and wisdom of his words sink in.

Ways of Building A Relationship With Our Feelings

After reading Rumi's poem, reflect on which guest feeling may be showing up most for you now? When it knocks, what do you currently do? If you welcome it in, and give it space to Be, wonderful! You are honoring your feelings.

If not, what if the next time it arrives unannounced, you pause and thank it for caring enough to show up. Consider putting one hand on your heart, and asking it what it would like you to know…about your Self, the situation, or life. Then listen closely ♡

Consider journaling about whatever Feelings are arising for you during this holiday. Let your Self write for 10-15 minutes freestyle, without thinking about what you want to write, and nonstop. Use a timer if you like. Let your heart share freely without any judgement—trusting there is no right or wrong way to do this. Afterwards, if you like, read it and see if you discover something new or unexpected. Often there's a pearl or two revealed.

This week, notice which guest Feeling you have most difficulty welcoming in. Ask your Self what it is about this guest in particular that makes it difficult? Is it that you feel embarrassed or ashamed when this guest shows up; that you were taught a "nice" person shouldn't have such feelings; it is so uncomfortable; or that every time this guest arrives, his/her friend Fear is also there.

What is one small step you can take toward making this guest feel a bit more welcome... at least opening the door a crack.☺ Wonderful gifts come over time as we do!

_____

_____

_____

_____

Navigating Life Stress

"When your world moves too fast and you lose yourself in the chaos, introduce yourself to each color of the sunset. Reacquaint yourself with the earth beneath your feet. Thank the air that surrounds you with every breath you take. Find yourself in the appreciation of life."

— CHRISTY ANN MARTINE

31
What a Difference a Day Can Make

Often, we may experience an especially challenging day—perhaps due to an illness, accident or work situation. It may lead us to feeling overwhelmed, helpless and stressed, with 'what if' and other fearful thoughts. This may last one day, several days, or perhaps weeks. The reality is that we rarely know how the future will unfold, especially in times of uncertainty or crisis. Despite what we'd like to think of our Selves, we're not such great fortunetellers.

In times of such uncertainty and perhaps angst, I've discovered one of the best strategies is to **narrow our time frame.** By this, I mean taking things one day (or one week) at a time, and staying in the present as much as possible. We may notice our thoughts going into the future—trying to foresee, plan for worst case scenarios, and asking what if questions, which often just lead to increased anxiety and stress.

Several years ago my sweet dog Buddy got injured at the groomers, and was in a lot of pain. The first week was especially challenging, witnessing this and trying to find good pain management, and a more knowledgeable vet. There was one day in particular that was especially hard, with his road to recovery quite uncertain. I noticed my Self beginning to feel overwhelmed and stressed, not knowing what to do to help him. The next day, Buddy appeared slightly better—for no reason I could identify. Hope increased with some relief, and a renewed perspective. I was reminded again of how impossible it is to accurately predict the future, and how a single day can become a turning point….if we let it.

Letting a Day Make a Difference

Is there any area of your life now that is filled with uncertainty and worry? Perhaps it feels like a rollercoaster at times. On the more challenging days, notice your thoughts, and ask your Self "Are they in the past, present or future?" Bring your thoughts gently back to the present if they are not. Take some deeper breaths as you do.

Broaden your perspective. Consider this particular situation may last for a while, and that it might unfold more like a marathon than a sprint. This means it's even more important to practice good self-care, and to do things regularly that lift your spirits. Take breaks, find ways to laugh, get support. What will help you endure this with as much wellbeing as possible, and not suffer through?

Identify what's in your control and focus on taking those steps. One day at a time. This is especially important if you're feeling overwhelmed by it all. Give your Self some grace. You deserve it. Acknowledge what you've done, and don't forget to notice the little milestones and progress along the way!

This week, consider one area of your life that may feel very uncertain and difficult at times? Ask your Self, "What tilt in perspective can I consider with this situation?" "How can I give my Self more grace and kindness in dealing with this in the weeks ahead? "What do I need today to feel supported and capable?" Listen closely, and be open to whatever wise, silly or unexpected inclination comes up. Then follow it, and notice the new possibilities that appear.

_____

_____

_____

_____

32
Assessing Your Stress

W hat I know for sure about stress is that it's insidious. Most of us don't realize just how stressed we are until we begin to develop symptoms. It could be tension in our shoulders or neck, a headache, stomach issues, becoming accident-prone etc. What makes it so hard to assess our stress level accurately? I often share with my coaching clients the frog-in-a-pot metaphor, which accurately describes what often happens to us. **It goes like this:** If you take a frog, and put it into a boiling pot of water, what do you think it will do? It will likely jump out of the pot, recognizing the danger. If you take the same frog, and put it in a lukewarm pot of water and slowly raise the temperature, what do you think it will do now? It will continue to swim around the pot, not realizing the water is getting very hot, until unfortunately it's too late. At times throughout our lives, we will be the frog.

In my own life and those of my clients, I repeatedly noticed this happening. **I attribute it to a phenomena,**

which I call "tolerance to stress." It refers to a phenomena in which we habituate to our current level of stress, and believe we are handling it well. Our current stress level could actually be a 6 out of 10 (10 being the highest), however because we've habituated over time, it feels more like a 4/10. Additional stressors develop, and we're now at an 8/10. We experience our stress level more like a 6/10 because we've become tolerant to it, and believe we are coping decently. Unfortunately, our bodies our not meant to handle high levels of stress (7/10 or above) for extended periods, and symptoms ultimately develop.

Ways to Better Assess Our Stress

It's important to know how moderate to high levels of stress begin to affect our body, minds, health, and relationships over time. Consider reading my book **From Stressed to Centered: A Practical Guide to a Healthier and Happier You.** The first few chapters include an overview on stress, including a comprehensive list of stress symptoms, and a brief inventory to better assess your current stress level. Whether you read this (or something else), knowing key stress symptoms is the first step in assessing it.

Reflect on your current wellbeing. Are you experiencing any stress-related symptoms? Some examples include overeating or eating very fast, difficulty sleeping, easily irritated, or trouble focusing. There are many additional symptoms.

If so, consider one small step you can take to increase your self-care behaviors.

This week, consider making a list of the top 2-3 current stressors in your life. Identify the one that you have the most control over. Is there a way to completely eliminate this stressor from your life? If not, what is one small action you can take to proactively begin to resolve or reduce this stressor? Then, do it, and notice the increased sense of control and peace you feel as you take this important action.

One of the best ways I've discovered to more accurately assess our stress is to look at our self-care practices. This is based on my professional life experience of over 20 years observing client behaviors. I also noticed a similar pattern personally in my own life. See Reflection #33.

_____

_____

_____

_____

33
What Stress Zone are You in?

What is the number one mistake most of us make when we're experiencing increased stress? **We decrease our self-care behaviors.** We tell our Selves we don't have enough time, need to focus on the increased responsibilities, or will do it next week. These may seem like reasonable responses to the additional demands on us. However, such responses are the opposite of what would help us deal most effectively with our rising stress. Sometimes we feel we don't have enough energy left for our self-care. This is a sure signal that our demands are exceeding our resources—and very likely our stress level has increased.

When we are under increased stress, the best strategy for our mental, emotional and physical well-being is to **increase our Self-care behaviors during this time.**

So, with some reverse engineering, we can assess our stress zone!

Your Stress Zone (based on Dr. Dana's Self-Care Inventory)

Green Zone: You are in this zone when life is going along relatively smoothly, you don't feel stressed and you're able to consistently maintain your daily and weekly self-care practices with relative ease (i.e., exercise, socialize with friends, play with your children, enjoy one or more hobbies).

Yellow Zone: In this zone, you are maintaining most of your self-care behaviors. However, it is becoming more difficult and you noticed that some of your regular self-care practices have begun to slip (i.e., your exercise has dropped from three to two days per week; you haven't played with your children/pet in days; quality time with your partner/friends has been rescheduled several times. You also have been experiencing some symptoms of stress lately.

Red Zone: You are in this zone when most, if not all, of your typical self-care practices have disappeared from your regular routine. For example, you realize you haven't done anything for your Self—workouts, time with family/friends, hobbies, meditation or spiritual practice—in weeks or months. You also feel stressed, and likely have experienced several symptoms, for an extended period of time.

Dana Gionta

This week, reflect on your self-care practices over the past several weeks. Have you noticed any changes? Does it seem harder to find the time or energy to do something for your Self? Are you experiencing any symptoms of stress?

If yes, consider which stress zone you're likely in. Then identify one self-care behavior you can do for your Self this week that would feel good and help center you. Make it a priority, and do it! Notice how you feel afterwards...perhaps energized, more focused, or peaceful.

_____

_____

_____

_____

34
Drama Rama All Around

Something we don't often talk about is how much drama may be in our lives. Many times, we're not aware of the chaos being drama. We perceive it as normal—this is the way our family, friends, or workplace just is. This happens because we are so close to the situation and the people involved, making it very difficult to see things objectively. Fortunately, there are signals that alert us to drama. **Feeling drained, stressed, confused, or having the urge to help, rescue, and put out frequent fires are very good signals that drama is in the room.** Get out now…before it's too late.☺

Some Important Questions:

How often do you have a conversation with someone in your life, and afterwards feel exhausted, frustrated or stressed?

Would you describe an environment in your life now as chaotic, roller coaster-like, crisis-oriented, or always problem-focused?

Are others frequently turning to you to complain, talk about their latest crisis, solve their problems, or be their forever cheerleader/therapist?

Does anyone in your life see himself/herself as a victim or a martyr? People with this issue are often draining and drama-oriented.

If the answer to any of the above is yes, you have drama rama going on in your life. This is important to become aware of, as ongoing drama significantly affects our energy, wellbeing, ability to focus on our own lives and priorities, and takes up much of our valuable time.

Some Ways to Address Drama

Consider if there is anyone in your life now that you feel creates drama (can use the signals above). If so, reflect on how often you interact with this person, and the impact it is likely having on you (scale 1-10 highest). Scores of 6 and above warrant taking action now. This could include setting a boundary with this person, reducing the frequency of communication with him/her, or having an honest conversation with them about your relationship.

This week, bring increased awareness to your interactions with others in your life. Ask your Self how you feel—both during the conversation and afterwards. Do you often feel relaxed, positive, and have the same or better energy level? Do the conversations typically feel reciprocal? If so, wonderful! They are nourishing to you.

If not, consider one action you can take to protect your Self from the drama. Then go ahead, and do it, and notice the increased peace and well-being that follows.

_____

_____

_____

_____

Empower Your Self

"I embrace uncertainty and uncomfortable situations with courage. I face new experiences with my mind and heart wide open.
I choose growth and expansion."

— Moon Omens Team

35
Identify Your Limits

O ften times we are not aware of what our limits are—whether physical, emotional, mental, spiritual, or financial. Some people voice their opinions about our lives or choices, and make unreasonable expectations of us. Others hold us responsible for something that is not our responsibility, take advantage of us, do not treat us with respect, or show us little compassion when in pain. These could be our family members, friends, co-workers, bosses and even people we've just met. This happens for many reasons—the other person doesn't understand what respectful behavior is, has poor relationship boundaries or personality issues, or is insecure. More importantly, these behaviors continue because, for various reasons, we allow it. No judgment here… just compassion and curiosity with our Selves.

Our limits are what define us in relationship to someone or something. Our feelings help us to know when we've bumped into or reached our limit. They

are our boundary guides. Three key feelings that signal you have likely reached a limit are: discomfort, guilt, and anger/resentment.

Some Things to Consider about our Limits:

What if we were more clear about what our physical, emotional, mental, spiritual and financial limits are? How might we respond differently? For example, if you notice your Self feeling uncomfortable with the thought of lending money to a friend, recognize this is an emotional limit of yours, and honor it.

If you are experiencing any of the above behaviors by others, gently ask yourself, what is leading me to continue to allow this behavior?

This week, see if you can identify one limit—start small. Notice any repeated feelings of discomfort, guilt, or resentment in a particular relationship or area of your life. Perhaps you are being guided to set a boundary here. If so, take some imperfect action and set one!

_____

_____

_____

_____

36
Why Set Boundaries?

What happens when someone or something brings us to our limit—a feeling of repeated discomfort, guilt or anger/resentment. This is an opportunity to set a boundary. We can think of boundaries as our limits in action. To gain a better understanding of how to identify our limits, review the previous reflection #35 Identifying our Limits. Boundaries serve many valuable functions. They help protect us, preserve our physical and emotional energy, help us clarify what is and isn't our responsibility, create work/life balance and honor our needs, values and truth.

We can have boundaries, however they have no power to do any of the above, unless we choose to implement them. We do this by what we call setting a boundary. Setting boundaries is the way we communicate our limits to others, and in essence, put our limits into action. This respectfully lets others know what our limits are—in the form of healthy, open communication—and helps us honor the limits we have. This is empowering!

Several examples of when setting a boundary would be helpful:

- Your family members or friends have a habit of giving you their unsolicited opinions about every part of your life—parenting, lifestyle, weight, finances, past choices, etc. This makes you feel uncomfortable, irritated, and even angry at times. What do you do? Do you set a boundary, and let them know that although well-intentioned, their opinions about your life makes you feel uncomfortable and less than. You would appreciate it if they would save their opinions for the times you specifically ask for their advice.

- You are often asked to work during your lunch hour or into the evenings. You realize this is increasing your stress level and making you feel drained by the end of the day. What do you do? Consider setting a work/ life boundary by speaking with your boss about your current work demands, and how they are increasingly impacting your wellbeing, and your personal time, including lunch and evenings.

- Your clients call you during dinner hours, or late into the evenings. You notice you are starting to feel guilty for allowing this to affect your time with your family, and perhaps resentful toward the client who is not respecting your limits. Consider setting a boundary here. For example, you can let them know that you are available to speak until 6:30pm Monday through Friday, otherwise they can leave a message, and you will get in touch the next day.

This week, think about a relationship or situation which would benefit from setting a boundary. Ask your Self, how would setting a boundary make me feel...calmer, more in control, confident etc.?

Which boundary would you like to set?

_____

_____

_____

Rate on a scale from 1-10 (very difficult) how difficult or uncomfortable it feels to imagine setting the above boundary this week. _____

If starting to set boundaries feels very difficult, that's okay! Boundary setting is a skill that takes practice. The more we do it, and again—start small—the better we will get at it, and the less intimidating and easier it will be. Consider one to two possible obstacles that come up when you imagine setting a boundary.

Learning about boundaries and how to set them is an invaluable skill that will help you tremendously in your relationships, career and life.

Congratulate your Self for doing this exercise. And trust setting boundaries will get easier over time with practice, and will boost your confidence as well. How wonderful is that!

"Love yourself enough to set boundaries. Your time and energy are precious. You get to choose how you use it. You teach people how to treat you by deciding what you will and won't accept."

— ANNA TAYLOR

37
The How of Setting Boundaries

Previously, I described boundaries as our limits defining us in relationship to someone or something. Boundaries can be tangible and physical, like a fence outlining where your property ends, and your neighbor's begins. Personal physical boundaries include our bodies and our personal space.

Boundaries can also be intangible, which address emotional and mental aspects. An emotional boundary involves an interaction or situation that negatively affects our feelings and emotions in some way. It leads us to feeling sad, afraid, guilty, angry, or stressed. A boundary related to our mental well-being involves a judgment or an attack on our personal opinions, beliefs, values, life philosophy, or ways of seeing and experiencing the world.

How To Set Boundaries:

1. Begin by identifying your limits by paying close attention to your feelings. Discernment will come over time.

2. Once you've identified a limit, notice how often you are reaching this limit within a relationship or a situation. Observe the feelings that arise, and ask your Self what you specifically need in this situation to feel better.

3. If you determine a boundary needs to be set, do your best to communicate your limit in a respectful and matter-of-fact way.

Here are some examples of setting boundaries by respectfully communicating your limits:

- "I don't feel comfortable going to X place on the weekends because of the crowds. I'd like us consider other times during the week, or another activity for the weekends."

- "No, I am not able to attend the work function/party this Friday." It's very important to give ourselves permission to say no.

- "I feel I have been doing more than my part of this project over the past several weeks. I would like for us to review the responsibilities, and come up with a more equitable arrangement.

- "When you are about to share what you believe is good advice, I'd like you first to ask me, "How can I help?" before you give me your thoughts."

The above can apply to opinions also. Travel happens to be a passion of mine. Over the years, I've had a number of people share unsolicited opinions about what they perceive to be my "jet setting" lifestyle. There was no basis to this. It's important to remind your Self in these moments that such comments are more a reflection of the person (and perhaps their insecurities, unrealized dreams or envy etc.) than You.

This week, think of how setting a physical, emotional or mental boundary in one area of your life could be helpful. You can use the boundary you identified earlier from Reflection #36, if you like. Consider writing out what you want to say, and more importantly, get clear on what you need. Then practice setting that boundary out loud or with a trusted friend, coach or therapist. Remember, start small and build on the incremental successes!

_____

_____

_____

_____

38
Live Life on Your Own Terms

One of the biggest regrets people have as they are dying is that they didn't live the life they wanted. They often did what others expected of them, putting family, friends' and everyone else's needs above their own. Perhaps this happened because they weren't aware of what their needs and desires were. Many of us learn in childhood and through various life roles to put our needs last. We may have strong desires or wants, however, we don't feel worthy enough to truly have what we want, so we don't try. Many of us also feel guilty if we do consider our own needs in addition to others'. Sometimes, we were called selfish when we did try to care for our Selves.

Perhaps we don't feel strong enough to cope if we go for it, and don't succeed. How utterly disappointing that might be. Where would that leave us?

Experiencing these uncomfortable, even painful feelings, can lead us over time to unconsciously disconnect from our deepest needs and desires to protect our Selves.

We may have a niggling sense, a quiet voice whispering to us that this isn't the life we imagined for our Selves. That "I'm not living my own life." The life that I really want—whether that's traveling around the world, becoming an artist, finally getting that college degree, or having a child. Sometimes it presents itself through an area of our lives that brings repeated frustration and disappointment. It is important to pay attention to this quiet voice—our intuitive sense—that we are not living true to our Selves.

Considerations on Living Life On Your Own Terms

Reflect on how well you know your Self, what are your important needs? Write them down, and ask your Self, "How well am I meeting my own needs, as well as others'?" If there is a significant imbalance, notice this. Identify one action you can take to rebalance this, and better prioritize your own needs. Remember, a healthy balance is when we give as much importance to our needs as to others'.

What are 3-5 deep desires that you have? Are several of these a central part of the life you've imagined for your Self? If so, then these are likely deep desires of yours that merit your time and attention. With intention, take courageous action toward realizing them.

If you would like to live life more on your own terms, identify one to two obstacles you feel are blocking your ability to do so. Is it family or friends' expectations of you—to be there daily for them? Are there societal values and dictates of what success is that feel confusing, and distracting you from focusing on what your heart wants? Perhaps you have limiting beliefs that what you really want isn't possible for you?

This week, identify one action you can take that would feel aligned with the life you have imagined for your Self. Doing any of the above is a great start! It could be anything—a small step or even a leap—to bring you in the direction of your desired life. Let's go for it!

_____

_____

_____

_____

39
Connect With Your Power

There are times in our lives when we may feel helpless, hopeless, obligated, and unable to see our choices. This can lead us to feeling stuck. It could be a quality about ourselves or an area of our life that is difficult. During such times, it is challenging for us to see possibilities, and to recognize that we always have a choice. We forget about our inherent strengths and the resilience we've already shown throughout our lives—overcoming many obstacles. There is a tendency to give away our power to others—our family and friends' opinions, societal expectations/norms, and experts' advice.

We have choices in how we respond and the perspective we take. Our power lies in our ability to see our possibilities, and take actions that enhance our sense of Self. These choices lead us to feel stronger and empowered, not weaker or like a victim.

Ways to Connect with Our Power:

Strengthen your relationship with your Self each day. We can do this in many ways—through journaling, quiet time with our Selves, meditation, solo walks in nature, prayer, yoga, etc. My favorites: I journal using the morning pages technique, and read something uplifting for 15-20 minutes. I added a daily meditation about a month ago. I've found these practices invaluable in building a stronger relationship with my Self. Try one or two of these daily practices, and notice how more grounded you feel in your Self!

Practice reflecting on your possibilities in each situation. When you encounter a challenging decision, ask your Self, "What are my choices in this situation?" Come up with at least 3 ideas, with at least one feeling like a stretch! Practice thinking creatively. If you can't see any additional possibilities, consider doing one of the practices above, and asking the question again. Then listen closely.

Where are you placing your power—within your Self, or are you looking outward to others for guidance, advice, support? **Begin tuning in more to your own wisdom, and cultivate greater trust in yourself.** This will nurture a deeper connection with your inherent power.

Notice your language. Are the words you're speaking empowering, reflecting your ability to influence the situation. Or do they reflect a sense of self that is stuck in helplessness?

This week, as situations arise, ask your Self, "What possibilities do I have, either in my actions or perspective?" Let yourself be creative and have some fun with this, if possible. Connect with your power by choosing the possibility that feels most empowering! Then do it, and notice how good you feel about your Self afterwards!

_____

_____

_____

_____

40
Friendshifts

Throughout our lives, we will experience shifts in our friendships for many reasons—differing developmental stages, relocation, academic or career demands, illness etc. These are normal developmental or life changes that often impact our relationships. Most of us can understand friendshifts that might occur because of the above.

What is more difficult, and often painful, is when shifts in our friendships happen from other factors. Some of these include the realization that the friendship is not reciprocal, that there is jealousy and our friend cannot be happy for us, or that our friend is not happy in their life and is unwilling to take any proactive steps—resulting in negativity and a victim mentality. Sometimes it's a pattern of behavior (i.e. how they deal with anger) or an inability to communicate in a healthy, respectful way about your differences that contribute to a change of heart about the friendship.

Several years ago, I was faced with this reality with a friendship of over thirty years, whom I considered family. She had become increasingly unhappy in her life after a series of difficulties and refused to get professional help. She had looked to me to be her therapist instead, which is not wise for any of us to do in our personal lives. After several unsuccessful attempts to set healthy and loving boundaries in this relationship, I realized that it could not continue as is. Letting go of a friendship that is no longer healthy and positive for us takes courage. There was also real grief… with eventual relief, acceptance and peace.

Navigating Friendshifts

Consider if there is a friendship in your life that feels unsupportive and draining. Perhaps it's a mix of both, with laughter and comfort interspersed with negativity and imbalance. Bring increased attention to your interactions over the next month, noticing how you feel when together, and upon leaving. If more often drained or like a roller coaster, strongly consider taking a step back and giving your Self some space. This will allow a clearer perspective to inform your next steps.

If you have a friendship that is currently shifting, and find it confusing, stressful or painful—deeply know that you are not Alone. This is a life experience many others share. Experiment with what feels helpful in processing this shift. Some ideas include journaling about, sharing with another close friend, directly communicating with this friend about your feelings, being in nature, starting therapy, or even friendship therapy together to safely address the issues.

This week, reflect on your closest circle of friends. Identify which ones feel good, supportive, and healthy. Notice your energy when you're together, and what positive qualities they bring out in you. This is a wonderful gift. Then consider sharing with them how much you love and appreciate them, and what the friendship means to you. Just imagine the positive friendshifts such open-hearted expressions will create over time!

_____

_____

_____

_____

A Reflective Pause

Celebrate your Self for coming this far on your yearlong journey to Self-Love! I'm very happy for You—with this showing a beautiful commitment to yourself. Over the past several months, there's been additional concepts, practices and courageous steps taken, with likely new insights, and Self-discoveries along the way.

Below, I invite you to pause and:

Reflect on the last few months, and consider the following:

1. What concepts have you found most helpful so far? And why?

   _____

   _____

2. Which 1-3 practices have you integrated into your daily/weekly routine and how have they been helpful?

   _____

   _____

3. In what ways have you stretched your Self, and taken some courageous steps?

_____

_____

4. Share 2-3 favorite insights and Self-discoveries you've had.

_____

_____

Celebrate your Self for taking this time to reflect, for the courageous steps you've taken so far, and the small and larger ways you've blossomed over the past few months.

Taking Action

"Follow what brings you joy, that is where the magic is, and there is where you come alive. What have you longed to do and be? Decide that **now** is the time to gift the world with your magnificence. There is no turning back. You are a forward moving beam of light—a star."

— ULONDA FAYE, SUTRAS OF THE HEART: SPIRITUAL POETRY TO NOURISH THE SOUL

41
Don't Wait

Many times throughout our lives, we wait for what we want, hope or dream of. We wait for many reasons...until we have enough money in our accounts, retire, the children our grown, the parents are gone etc. Sometimes we wait because of fear, or we may not believe what we want is possible. We think to our Selves—one day I will do or have this. That day turns into 10 years later. As much and as comfortable as it is to believe that we have many years to eventually do or have what we desire, that is not the reality of life. What is true is that life is unpredictable, and the gift of living into our golden years is not guaranteed—for any of us. Life can be short. We often don't want to accept this truth, and we're very adept at avoiding it. Nonetheless, it is reality. **It takes much courage to face the realities of life (no matter what situation we find our Selves in).**

I learned this truth at a relatively young age, with my parents' death, and then the death of a close friend of mine at age 59. There have been a handful of others over the years. Death and illness bring this truth repeatedly to light. These are the unexpected gifts of both. Each can guide us to live our lives more vibrantly—if we let them. Let them….

So, if there is something important that you've been wanting to do, a heart's desire, a passion you'd like to pursue, a new lifestyle/career, a dream to go after, then don't wait any longer. Begin now, whatever that may look like for you. Just start. Take one small step, then another. You may even find your Self leaping! Wonderful!☺ Do whatever it takes to begin. Don't let your Self live passively, waiting for whatever it may be. Get in the driver's seat, step on the gas, and go after what you want (with fear along for the ride!). I'm here cheering you on!!

Have an adventure, some new experiences, and discover more of your Self along the way. I've taken some courageous leaps over the past several years, and they all have been worth it! And scary! But that is the nature of change, and going after what's important to us.

From Waiting to Getting in the Driver's Seat

Ask your Self if there's something you've been truly wanting to do, or a heartfelt desire you've put off for awhile. Perhaps it's something you really want in your life but are afraid you'll never get, so you don't even try. To risk and fail seems worse. It's not. What's worse is ongoing regret. Then write down whatever this heartfelt desire is, and how long you've been wanting this. Reflect on how important this is to you, and how you would feel if whatever it is happened.

Brainstorm with your Self (or others) about making what you desire real. What are some possibilities? Let your Self be creative and imagine whatever comes to mind. List 5 possible, even outlandish, ways you can move toward having what you want.

This week, consider how waiting for what you want or not trying has affected you. Then identify one small step you could take while in the driver's seat, in the direction of whatever it is you truly desire. Congratulate your Self and notice how you feel as you begin taking those steps.

_____

_____

_____

_____

42
Clarity Comes Through Action

Often we believe that we can "think" our way to clarity. We may spend months, even years, trying to gain clarity about something—what direction to go in, what career to pursue, whether to marry this person, or how to get our finances in order. This deliberating, and sometimes even agonizing over, often comes at a high price—lost time and unnecessary suffering. We unconsciously stay in our heads instead of acting, because it feels safer. Sometimes we believe that we are indeed taking action because we are busy mentally problem-solving, journaling or talking with others repeatedly about our dilemma. This is not action, this is an illusion.

What if, instead, we make a self-loving decision, to get out of our head and onto our feet! We move in whatever direction we think is the next best step, or listen to what our intuition may be guiding us to do. Trust your Self. Then we give it some time, and reflect on how we feel on this new path. Do we notice more energy, enthusiasm and peace? These are all positive signs that the steps we're taking are in the right direction. There may be a detour or two ahead, but we're gaining greater clarity (and feedback) with each step.

Some Things to Consider on our Path Toward Clarity

There is an important principle in the area of effective leadership. It is to balance thinking (or planning) with taking action. Too much planning can lead to delayed action, and acting too quickly with little thought can result in undesired outcomes. The key is balance. We can also apply this principle to our Selves—as we lead our own lives.

Sometimes we know it is time to take action, yet we cannot bring ourselves to begin, because of fear, perfectionism, indecision as to how or where to start etc. One of the best things you can do then is to seek support to help you move forward—whether that's speaking to a close friend or family member, a trusted co-worker, or a professional coach or therapist. Who will you reach out to?

Trust that greater clarity will come, even if we presently feel like we're wading through a swamp and can't see a thing. Take a step, then another. **Action creates momentum.** No action leads to stagnation. You will receive feedback with each step, as you move beyond your comfort zone, and further develop your self-trust and confidence. All good things! Remember, this is a judgment-free path.♡

This week, consider one area of your life where you would like greater clarity. Ask your Self, "How long have I been thinking about this?" And, "Have I taken any real action over the past several months in this area?" If not, what has stopped me?

Then, identify one action you can take, and start the positive momentum forward by taking it!

_____

_____

_____

_____

43
Give Yourself Permission

W hy do we often need to give ourselves permission? Because many times in our life, and often each day, we desire to do something (or not to) and we talk our Selves out of it. It usually starts with "I shouldn't because" or "What if" or "If I don't do it, something unpleasant or uncomfortable is going to happen." We are often unconsciously conditioned by the environments we're in—whether that is our broader culture, ethnic norms, family backgrounds, workplace etc. In addition, there is also much messaging we receive about what is and is not possible for women, and how a woman "should" be or act. For example, we often hear a nice woman doesn't do X.

This powerfully came to my awareness within the first year of relocating to Vegas. I began sensing that my downstairs neighbor, who was living with his partner at the time, had more than a neighborly interest in me. My intuition was also telling me that he likely had some type of addiction. One night, about 9:30pm I get a loud knock on my door. My dog Buddy jumped out of his bed, and and I was quite startled. My first thought was "who is knocking on my door at this hour?" I asked who it was, and this neighbor answered that he saw the empty boxes I had on my landing to discard, and that he would throw them away for me.

I could sense that he wanted me to open the door, since he's doing this apparent kind neighborly act for me. My intuition, however, quickly told me a very different reality. That if I opened that door, I wouldn't be able to close it. He would insert his foot in the door, and force his way in. This was clearly quite scary and somewhat disorienting, as he had never previously made any aggressive gesture. Yet, despite this crystal clear intuition, my conditioning as a woman was that you open the door and thank someone if they're doing some thing nice for you. It was incredible to observe this conflict of knowing (based on my intuition) and doing (based on years of conditioning as a woman)... happening at such a critical moment.

I decided to trust my intuition, and give my Self full permission to break societal norm and be considered rude—and not open the door. He immediately reacted with anger when I didn't , and I knew then with 100% certainty that my intuition was right! So, sometimes, giving your Self permission can powerfully protect You. And listening to your intuition! ♡

Perhaps You've Been Wanting To:

- Take a break, and carve out more time for your Self each day.

- Go back to school and begin taking classes in something you feel excited about.

- Speak to your boss about an ongoing issue you're having at work.

- Find a way to travel more, and have new adventures.

- Take up a new hobby you think you'll enjoy or resume doing something you know you love.

- Start a side business that you love.

- Tell a friend or family member their attempts at being helpful are not helpful to you. Instead, "this is what I would really find helpful at this time…"

The first step in making any of the above happen is to listen to your Self, acknowledge what you need, then give your Self a beautiful gift…your permission. See what wonders begins to unfold.

Try it this week! And if you need a little help, you definitely have Dr. Dana's permission also! ☺

Faith & Beyond

"Faith does not need to push the river because faith is able to trust that there is a river. The river is flowing. We are in it."

– RICHARD ROHR

44
Never Give Up

O ften, our goals and dreams may feel out of our reach or perhaps even impossible.

This is the 10th year of my journey toward vibrant health. With much gratitude, I'm getting close! It has, like many things in life, been a winding trail—with detours, bumps, on the edge frightening moments, discouragement, tears, failures and ... wonder, joy, excitement, relief, renewed hope, perseverance, determination & courage.

At the time, I didn't believe some of the health changes were possible, like losing more than 5 lbs—since I had tried unsuccessfully for years!! I never would have believed that I could lose 35 lbs, and be the lightest I've been in 30 years. I thought this was truly impossible—far beyond what I could have imagined for my Self. Experiencing that this was indeed possible has been an invaluable life experience for me.

To get to this place of renewed health, I had to make major changes—to my lifestyle, way of eating, mindset, opening to alternative ways of healing/medicine, self-care and relationships. Most of these took courage... more than I realized in those moments. Only looking back do I see how courageous many of them were. **How much they required me to get out of my comfort zone and let go of conditioned ways of thinking.** One of the many health changes I made was to significantly reduce sugar in my life. Then later, I eliminated most gluten & dairy.

I've come to believe that living our lives more vibrantly involves cultivating a loving and trusting relationship with our Selves, developing a kind relationship with Fear, and often making courageous changes. With such changes, inevitably comes greater confidence—an unexpected and beautiful gift!

Ways to Move Toward The "Impossible"

What goals do you have that you've been afraid to move toward, perhaps tried but not succeeded, or have no idea how to begin? Ask your Self, "How long have I been wanting to do or have this? And "How important is this to me?" Reflect on **why** this is important to you, and how your life would be different if you were to reach your goal or start moving toward your dream.

Consider if there is a hidden belief you may have that whatever you most hope for is impossible. Take 3 minutes on your own, without distraction, and imagine actually reaching that goal. Notice what feelings and thoughts arise as you do. Were they mostly positive—or did self-doubt, fear, and more negative thinking arise? If negative, just bring curiosity and compassion to them.

This week, identify one goal you have that is important to you and that you would feel excited to move toward and ultimately reach! Identify one small action step you can take that feels like a positive start. Remember, it is action that creates motivation—and I dare say, inspiration! Perhaps it is reaching out for support (from a friend, co-worker or coach) or talking with others who have been successful in achieving a similar goal.

Look for a mentor too!

A Note of Encouragement

If any of you are also on this journey back to renewed health, don't give up!! Keep trying, experimenting, learning about your Self, talking to others who have been successful, & opening to various forms of healing. Reach out for support. And connect with your courage and faith. And remember, unsuccessful attempts do not mean failure. They are a signal to try another way! ♡

_____

_____

_____

_____

45
The Hidden Gifts of Deciding

We can think about something for weeks, months or even years before acting. Our thinking often shifts forms—to worrying, analyzing, deliberating, and even obsessing to the point of distraction. We call this chronic thinking about the same thing rumination. Our rumination is often insidious. It can deceive us into thinking we're effectively problem-solving about whatever situation or concern we have…when we're really not.

By delaying making a decision that is important, **we are in effect deciding to maintain the status quo.** We are choosing our comfort zone and what feels safe and known, over the risk of change. However, by not intentionally choosing, we often find our Selves in the land of limbo and continued rumination. Over time, this creates stress and becomes unhealthy.

Deciding is an act. Choosing one direction over another is powerful, and empowering. With intentional action comes greater clarity as each step gives us valuable information. **We are in a state of movement.** Stretching, growing, moving beyond our comfort zone—in the process of self-discovery. These are just some of the wonderful gifts of deciding!

Some Ways to Choose to Decide

- Notice how you are in making decisions. Do you decide quickly, often deliberately, or let others make the decision for you? That's also a decision. If so, select one small matter that you've been thinking about, and choose to act. Say "I decide…." There is power in this phrase.

- Make a list of several situations or matters that you've been deliberating about. For each one, write down how long you've been thinking about this. What actions have you taken? If none, that is okay. No judgment. Bring curiosity as to what may be contributing to your continued deliberations?

This week, select one of the above situations on your list. If you were to make a decision about this, what choices or directions are there? Identify the one that feels the best—brings a sense of peace or empowerment. Then act by deciding to move in that direction, one step at a time.

Congratulate your Self for deciding! Notice the positive shift in your energy as you move forward, with faith and courage as your companions—and out of the realm of rumination.

_____

_____

_____

_____

46
Are You Open To Receiving?

The etymology of the word receive is "to get, take hold of, welcome and accept." Often, we find it easier to give than to allow our Selves to receive. Whether it's a compliment, a friendly gesture of opening the door for us, or buying us a cup of coffee—we often politely reject it. By giving more often than we allow our Selves to receive, we deny our Selves and others the gift of kindness and generosity.

What is it about receiving that might feel uncomfortable, even scary? Is it that we learned early on that if we receive, then we "owe" others something in return...a future favor? Perhaps we feel like we don't deserve to receive because we are not worthy enough. Often, we have underlying beliefs that limit our openness to receiving. **I've come to believe that how accepting we are of our Selves influences our ability to accept from others. If we are kind and giving** to our Selves, it is easier and more comfortable to allow others to be kind and generous to us.

Some Ways to Allow our Selves to Receive

Look for opportunities of receiving that often occur each day. It could be a kind gesture from someone, a feeling of joy that arises, an experience of beauty that catches your breath, or someone's smile in your direction. Then notice your typical response and feelings—are you often accepting or more declining, comfortable or uneasy in some way?

Give your Self permission each day to allow yourself to receive something small…whatever that may be. Then express some gesture of gratitude, whether a simple thank you, or feeling grateful for a smile received. Being in Nevada, I am open to receiving the incredible gifts of beautiful sunsets daily, and unexpected visits from precious hummingbirds.

Let go of any beliefs you become aware of that limit your openness to receiving, especially the belief of being indebted to someone if you accept something. This is a tit for tat way of thinking that doesn't serve anyone.

This week, reflect on your current level of openness to receiving. Ask your Self, What would I really like to allow my Self to receive? List 3-5 things or experiences. Take a few minutes and visually imagine receiving something on your list. Notice what feelings arise, and how your body feels as you are receiving this. Give your Self this gift in the year ahead, and watch your experiences of joy and open-heartedness increase.

_____

_____

_____

_____

47
A Heart Awakening

find much joy in writing regularly and for my community, and I realized last year I needed to honor my limits, and pause this. I hope my story below may help one or more of you in your health journey, and perhaps even be life-saving.

In March, on a very ordinary day, my life shifted. I went for my yearly physical, and returned for the results a week later. I was told quite nonchalantly that my EKG was abnormal, and that it showed I had a previous silent heart attack. I heard him say the words, however, I didn't believe it. My heart felt fine, nothing unusual over the past few years. Still, a little unsettling…

A week later, a cardiologist did a repeat EKG. Same exact results. I was quite surprised and now concerned. What if this is true? Could this happen again, when, and with what impact the next time? I was sent for an echocardiogram and stress test to evaluate further. It had now been about 3 plus weeks waiting to know if I did indeed have a silent heart attack. Any of you who've had health issues understand the emotional rollercoaster involved with waiting.

Over the past 20 years, I've struggled with various health issues, some quite significant. I discovered that there is something unique about feeling like you could have a heart attack, at any moment, with no notice. Perhaps it's having very little control over the possibility of another heart attack that contributes to feeling quite vulnerable.

After additional testing, I learned that I very fortunately did Not have a silent heart attack, but they did detect moderate blockage in the main artery to my heart, aka "the widow-maker," kindly shared by the doctor. This was eye-opening and unnerving. For more than a decade I was informed by my doctors that my high cholesterol was not really a problem. Not high enough to be concerned about heart disease etc.

Over the past 5 months, I needed time… to process what had happened and to research and begin educating myself about heart disease, high cholesterol, risk factors and how to prevent and reverse existing coronary artery disease. All this informed my decision to transition to whole food plant-based (WFPB) eating, which involved eliminating dairy, and significantly reducing saturated fats. (I love cheese as much as I love chocolate, so no cheese for 2 months! Say whaaat?)

I also spent time finding WFPB foods and recipes, including healthy cheese-like substitutes, that were easy to make—and that I would actually enjoy eating on a regular basis. Later in my journey, I happily discovered Yoga Nidra, a wonderful practice that I do several times per week, that has deep relaxation and restorative benefits. I highly recommend you give it a try!

The Light of Courageous Change:

Often with most crises, there are unexpected blessings. I found some delicious recipes and discovered how much I enjoy WFPB eating. What a lovely surprise!! I also discovered my sleep is much better, and noticed improved energy, skin and even mood after a few weeks of doing. Another incredible blessing was the heartwarming show of love and support from friends and family. This made a real difference in my heart journey.

And last but not least, the results of eating WFPB on my cholesterol levels were quite impressive to both my total cholesterol and LDL, after only 2 months! I now feel more empowered with greater knowledge and confidence in maintaining a healthy heart.

Ways of Awakening to Your Heart

Make some time for stillness. Consider if there's a Pause in some area of your life that your heart is longing for you to take. Perhaps there's an area that's causing some stress or affecting your peace of mind?

This week, bring increased attention to the whisperings of your heart. Consider asking your heart if there's any longing yet to be realized, or perhaps some healing needed. Then listen closely, and notice any images, memories or feelings that come to you. This is an intuitive way to connect more closely with your heart.

Valuable lesson:

Sometimes we need to significantly Pause what we're doing and intentionally create greater time and space to reflect, heal and evaluate our best next steps. Trusting my intuition, and having faith that my connection with my community would not be significantly impacted allowed me to honor my need for a Pause.

Heart health tip:

If you have moderate to high cholesterol levels (or a family history of heart disease or diabetes), ask your doctor for a Cardiac calcium test to assess the degree of calcium buildup in the arteries of your heart. Moderate to high levels of calcium place you at increased risk of a potential heart attack or stroke.

Let Go of Perfection and Get Unstuck

"The activity you're most avoiding contains your biggest opportunity."

- Robin S. Sharma

48
The Opposite of Self-Acceptance

We all want to belong, be accepted, and feel loved. Often, we come to believe that if we are flawless, then others will accept us, and we won't be rejected or abandoned. Unknowingly, we begin striving for perfection, creating unreasonably high standards for our Selves, rather than accepting where and who we are in this moment. We are a mosaic of wonderful qualities, talents, strengths, quirks, passions—and vulnerabilities, limitations and flaws. However, wearing the lens of perfectionism, we often only see what is not 100%, what is not "right" with us. As we focus on this, we move further away from embracing all of who we are with acceptance and compassion.

What if, instead, we choose to strive for our best, instead of perfection, and allow our Selves to accept where we are now. We can give our Selves permission to be human and make mistakes, to take imperfect action, to fall moving forward—and learn from it all with humor, kindness and even appreciation for the process. What if it was okay to fail, to flounder, to be vulnerable, to look silly, and to just be and not do sometimes. Can you sense the freedom and acceptance in this, and the gentle and loving regard we might come to feel for our Selves?

Reflect on where you might have first observed and experienced perfectionism. For many, including myself, it was often in childhood where we learn to have such impossible standards for our Selves. In my family, getting A's in school was just expected, not perceived as any particular accomplishment. Consider some implicit or direct messages you may have learned in your family. What more realistic, kind standards can you begin to replace them with?

Identify one area of your life perfectionism may be present, perhaps parenthood, marriage, career, Self, or friendships. A hint: Notice which area elicits the most judgment and pressure on your Self. Bring increased awareness to when the judgements arise, notice them with compassion, and then ask your Self what would be a kinder way to view this moment. What would doing your best—exactly as you are now—look like, rather than perfection? Then go ahead and make that your new standard!

This week, consider how perfectionism might be serving you in your life. Reflect on any benefits you can see, and in what ways it may be holding you back. Is perfectionism negatively affecting your sense of Self and relationships? Identify one perfectionistic tendency you do now, and allow your Self to give 85% instead. You have my permission. What would that look like?

Imagine the incredible freedom and joy you'll experience as imperfect action becomes your new way!

_____

_____

_____

_____

49
What Are You Avoiding?

There are times in our lives when facing a truth may feel too difficult. Perhaps it is a long-term friendship that is no longer nurturing, a health issue that has returned, disrespectful treatment by a colleague/boss, financial debt that is increasing, or the realization that you're not really happy. It can be quite uncomfortable and scary, maybe even terrifying, to acknowledge the truth about something in our lives that is important to us. The thought of potentially losing something that we care deeply about, or that a significant change may be required to improve the situation, can make us feel very uncomfortable. Sometimes facing the truth requires a major shift in our identity, and how we've come to define our Selves.

What I've often shared with my coaching and therapy clients over the years is that one of the most courageous things we will ever do is to face the reality—the truth—of a situation. However, many of us in the interim, while we're gathering up the courage and developing our inner strength and compassion, avoid it. No judgment here. This is a very human response, with much research to support the approach/avoidance pattern we all do at times.

Transforming Avoidance into Courage

Consider one aspect of your life, such as a relationship that makes you feel uncomfortable, anxious, and hesitant to talk about it. Notice if there are any feelings of shame or judgment around this. If so, allow your Self to acknowledge such feelings, and bring some compassion and kindness to your Self instead. Taking a moment to do this is already an act of courage!

We cannot face what we are unwilling to first glimpse. Reflect on what you've realized you have been avoiding, and give your Self permission to share it with a close friend or loved one who is nonjudgmental. If it feels better, reach out to a coach or therapist. This is also courageous… way to go!

If you cannot think of anything you may be avoiding, consider asking a trusted friend or family member for his/her perception of one thing you may be avoiding. Those around us can often see our situation—a blind spot—more clearly than our Selves at first.

This week, bring increased attention to any behavior(s) that supports avoiding whatever situation you have identified. Just notice the behavior and give your Self compassion, and even praise for how creative you've been to be so successful in your avoidance.☺ Imagine the wonder and confidence that will arise when you shift toward courageous action!

_____

_____

_____

_____

50
Practice Makes ?

Many of us grew up hearing the common expression "practice makes perfect." When we hear something enough times, we begin to believe it… even if it's not true. Can we ever really become perfect at something? Isn't there always more to learn and hone whatever skill we're developing? Much fear and procrastination comes from believing we need to be perfect. Such high and unrealistic standards often set us up to fail, or even worse, not try—because of the overwhelming fear that arises when we think of doing something.

What if instead, we think of practice another way. The other day I was taking a continuing ed class to overcome one of my own fears and the instructor reframed the expression to "practice makes proficient" or perhaps even better, "practice makes professional." I loved this, as I believe this more accurately reflects the true value and parameters of practice. This more realistic belief sets us up for success, and creates space for joy in the process of learning, for mistakes, and equally important, for our humanness. Let's give our Selves the gift of compassion whenever we are stepping out of our comfort zone and trying something new or scary.

Ways to Embrace Professional not Perfect:

Consider one way perfectionism is showing up in your life now. We may find ourselves avoiding, controlling or repeatedly doing something as a strategy to cope with the uncomfortable feelings our need to be "perfect" creates. Reflect on which coping strategy from the above you most often use.

Imagine giving your Self complete permission to do something MESSY! That's the only expectation… it may very well come out messy, and that's Ok, and perhaps you may surprise your Self. The only way to really know is to try it. Identify one thing you know you'd like to try if the outcome really didn't matter. Trust that as you practice it, you will become more proficient over time, and gain more confidence in the process and your Self.

This week, reflect on what practice you would like to perhaps start, resume or become more consistent at. Notice whatever feelings arise, especially discomfort, as you imagine doing any of the above.

Then connect with your courage and compassion, let go of the outcome, and begin. You'll be surprised at the wonderful things that will unfold when you do!

_____

_____

_____

_____

51
Embrace Imperfect Action

Most of us hold our Selves to a very high standard. Not just excellence, or doing our best—we want perfection. We evaluate ourselves by this marker, and often fall short. How can we not? This often leads us to feeling bad, and judging our Self as a "failure." Over time, we become afraid—to take a risk, make a mistake, go beyond our comfort zone. In essence, we become afraid to act. This is a real injustice—to our extraordinary Selves, to others, and to our larger communities. We all have unique talents, dreams, personalities, perspectives, and ways of approaching life that could enhance our lives and the world. Yet, we often let fear of not being perfect hold us back.

What if instead, we give our Selves permission to **take imperfect action.**

To be imperfect… as we grow. And, if we make a mistake, the only self-talk we say is: "What can I learn from this?" "How can I do it differently in the future and move closer to my goal?" That's it. Not, "I shouldn't have done it that way." Or "Why did I do that?" Or "That was foolish."

We can even get a little wild, and imagine giving our Selves credit for mustering up the courage, and just trying it! Whatever the outcome, we did it! That's to be celebrated.

What if we make it a practice to let go of worrying about the outcome, and just aim to do our best, with whatever knowledge and skill level we have now.

How might the experience of taking action be different? I imagine we might begin to like (even find enjoyment in) taking risks, and trying new things! And feel proud of our Selves, with increased confidence.

This week, take one imperfect action (start small) with the aim of doing the best you can in the moment, with whatever energy level, attention, and motivation you have. Then celebrate your progress rather than perfection!

_____

_____

_____

_____

52
Take A Risk

ften we are afraid to take a risk and do something different, or pursue what we really want. What if we fail? What if others disapprove or think it's foolish? Notice the "what if" nature of these thoughts. Other questions that come up: Do we deserve to have what we really desire? Who do we think we are to take a chance? If we risk and fail, then are we a failure? Many fearful thoughts often arise as we consider moving outside our comfort zone. That's part of our human condition. No judgment. However, they are just thoughts. They have as much or as little power as we give them.

Let's choose the questions we ask our Selves carefully.

"What if" questions and others can also encourage us to take that risk—rather than foster fear. For example, "What if I risk and succeed in moving closer to my goals and dreams? What new and wonderful things could I discover about my Self in the process of trying?" "Does failing at something really mean I am a failure?" "How true is that?"

Every time we take a risk, regardless of the outcome, we grow. This happens more quickly if we don't judge our Selves for the outcome.

Wonderings About Risk:

Consider doing something you've been afraid to do. It could be anything. Perhaps trying a new hobby, like drawing or baking; making a lifestyle change; eating healthier; setting a boundary; or sharing your feelings with a loved one. You can start small and give your Self encouragement.

Ask your Self, "How would I feel if I connected with my courage and took this risk? And it went well. What would this mean to me? Could this bring me a step closer to living my best life…and becoming my best Self?

Now let's face your fear about taking a risk. Reflect on what trying and 'not succeeding' would mean for you. What benefits could come from our trying? How may we grow and discover important aspects about our Selves through this?

We often learn more from our failures
than our successes…

This week, identify one thing you've wanted to try but felt afraid to do. Imagine your Self actually doing it, fear and all, for 2 to 3 minutes.

Get as visual as you can. Then go ahead and take the risk! Notice how you feel immediately after...perhaps proud of your Self and more empowered? Wonderful!!

_____

_____

_____

_____

Some Personal Experiences with Taking Risks

ay you find the stories below inspiring and perhaps affirming for you… ♡

Writing a book

By 2011, I began seeing how transformative my work with clients on self-care and boundaries was and had a growing desire to have a larger impact than one woman at a time. A colleague and friend of mine had expertise in stress management, and one day I mentioned to him, "Why don't we write a book together?"

It was exciting to think about the positive impact a book on stress management, self-care and boundaries could have. However, neither one of us was prepared for the numerous challenges, overwhelm and discomfort the journey of writing a book brings. There was a huge learning curve related to writing, editing, compiling it into a book, and deciding on self-publishing or traditional marketing, sales, and promotion.

This was a whole new world to both of us, and much uncertainty and fear came up throughout. It took significant courage, self-trust, support, determination, and a strong Why to sustain us over the three years it took to complete and publish it in 2014.

A sabbatical I took in Costa Rica

In 2014, I felt restless and questioned whether I was experiencing burnout in my practice of many years. During this time, I was also diagnosed with a potentially life-threatening health condition, which required surgery. My whole being longed for a break and to be near nature.

I decided to close my practice for two-plus months to take a well-needed sabbatical to heal and restore my Self in Costa Rica. It involved risking losing all of my clients and my practice. Fear again rose up. However, going through a frightening health issue and surgery and closing my practice in 2010 gave me the courage to take this risk. It was one of the best decisions I've made so far. I returned renewed, energized, and happy to resume my practice!

From entrepreneur to organizational life

In 2019, an opportunity to work in an organization affiliated with a well-known university came up. I would be able to use some additional talents, such as teaching and leadership coaching, and the salary and benefits would be excellent. It required me to close my business of thirteen years in CT, say good-bye to all my clients, and relocate to RI.

I had felt like I wanted a change and to challenge myself professionally in different ways. However, it felt like a tremendous risk—letting go of the security and benefits of having my own business, schedule, and wonderful clients, and starting a position working for an organization. After much consideration, I decided to take the risk. There was significant fear about making this change. Some feelings of grief to process around my clients, and the closing of my business.

After four to five months in the new position, I realized I would not be able to use those key talents I was excited about applying. Despite several attempts to set boundaries and address expectations with leadership, the continued lack of autonomy and minimal work/life balance was very difficult and draining.

After much reflection and acceptance of the reality of my situation, I made the very difficult decision to resign at one year. One of the many gifts that came from this tough period was the renewed appreciation and excitement to relaunch my business—with new services that utilized my broader talents and passions.

An Author's Note

I t's my heartfelt hope that, like a beautiful garden, you experienced your Self blossoming into the Loving woman you desire to be over the year long journey you courageously took.

This is not an ending. A new beginning is now unfolding! May this greater Self-love and confidence you now have allow you to shine your light brightly in this world, and bring you much happiness, peace and blessings in the years ahead…

About Dana Gionta

D ana Gionta, Ph.D. is a psychologist, professional speaker, executive coach and co-author of the book *From Stressed to Centered: A Practical Guide to a Healthier and Happier You.* She is the founder and CEO of Dana Gionta LLC. and specializes in work/life boundaries, courageous leadership, employee wellbeing and burnout, and organizational performance.

With a diverse professional background and experience spanning 20 years in business, psychology, coaching and health, Dana works with executives and high-achieving women in small to Fortune 500 organizations and family businesses. Clients come from many professions, including business, law, hospitality, medicine, education, the arts, and biotech. In her life coaching and psychology practice, she works with individuals on areas related to relationships, career challenges, boundaries, wellbeing and stress, and midlife transitions.

Dr. Gionta has been featured in Strategy + Business, Inc., Psychology Today, Inverse, PsychCentral, Expert Beacon and Lawline. She is also a columnist for the Psychology Today blog. Dr. Dana speaks nationally on topics related to boundaries in the workplace, employee well-being, work/ life balance, and burnout and self-renewal. A sample of Dana's client presentations include: Bic, FedEx, Brown University, Northeastern University, the American Institute of Architects, and Women in Dentistry.

Visit www.danagionta.com to learn more.

Other Ways to Stay Connected!

- https://www.linkedin.com/in/danagiontaphd/
- **Living Your Best You Newsletter**—Sign up at: https://danagionta.com/newsletter or visit www.danagionta.com
- Instagram: @danagiontacoaching

Will You Be A Part Of Something Special?

I would love for you to be a part of my Global *52 Weeks to Self-Love* BookTeam. It truly takes a village of amazing women to help spread the word and bring this book to the world.

7 Ways You Can Be a Part of my *52 Weeks to Self-Love* Village:

- Share the book on social media. My challenge is to sell 5,000 books (and hopefully more), so you can post a photo of you holding the book on Instagram, Facebook, or LinkedIn with your comments and the hashtags #52WeekstoSelf-Love, #selflove, and tagging me @danagiontacoaching

- Write a review of the book on Amazon, if purchased through it, or Goodreads. This will be incredibly helpful with the algorithms which makes a huge difference in helping other women find the book online.

- Share the book with friends, colleagues, and your networks. Recommend it to others and encourage them to visit the book page online or in bookstores. Would you be willing to include a short recommendation in your newsletter or mailings?

• Buy a book for a friend, loved one or colleagues! I hope you consider getting it for someone who may need inspiration, wants a deeper sense of self-love and confidence, or for someone who is interested in spirituality, self-care, or leading an authentic and heart-centered life.

• Share the book with a podcast host. Do you know anyone whose podcast is looking for inspirational speakers? Please let them know about me and the book.

• Do you like to do interviews? I'm happy to be inter-viewed for your show or webinar about topics related to the book, self-acceptance, courageous living, work/life boundaries, creativity, and more.

• Share the book with your book club and invite me to speak to them about it. I'd love to answer "behind the scenes" questions about the book, some of the personal stories I shared within it, and provide some greater depth of wisdom and strategies to your favorite reflections.

• Here's a BIG ASK! Would you like to sponsor a read-ing and book signing event, perhaps in collaboration with others? If you'd be willing to sponsor an event, that would be wonderful and most appreciated! You can contact me at danagionta.com.

I would love to hear from you!!

I t would bring me much joy if you connect with me and share your thoughts, feelings, and stories about how any part of *52 Weeks to Self-Love* was helpful to you—and brought more Self-love, confidence, peace and wellbeing to your life.

This was my heartfelt intention for this book.

Ordering information:

Special rates are available on quantity purchases by corporations, associations, and others.

For details, please direct inquiries to dr.gionta@gmail.com or visit www.danagionta.com.

For Speaking, please contact Dr. Dana through her website www.danagionta.com

Other Books
By
Dana Gionta, Ph.D.

From Stressed to Centered: A Practical Guide to
a Healthier and Happier You

www.ingramcontent.com/pod-product-compliance
Lightning Source LLC
Chambersburg PA
CBHW071154130626
46553CB00004B/1654